INDIVIDUARIAN OBSERVATIONS

INDIVIDUARIAN OBSERVATIONS

Essays in Catholic Social Reflection

William J. Byron, S.J.

UNIVERSITY OF SCRANTON PRESS
Scranton and London

© 2007 University of Scranton Press

All rights reserved.

Library of Congress Cataloging-in-Publication Data

Byron, William J., 1927-
Individuarian observations: essays in Catholic social reflection/William J. Byron.
  p. cm
Includes bibliographical references.
ISBN 978-1-58966-131-8 (pbk.)
1. Christian sociology—Catholic Church. I. Title.
BX1753.B97 2007
261.8—dc22

2007010401

Distribution:

University of Scranton Press
Chicago Distribution Center
11030 S. Langley
Chicago, IL 60628

PRINTED IN THE UNITED STATES OF AMERICA

For
Morey and Sondra Myers...
who have a way of making good things happen.

Also by William J. Byron, S.J.

Toward Stewardship (1975)
The Causes of World Hunger (editor, 1982)
Quadrangle Considerations (1989)
Take Your Diploma and Run (1992)
Take Courage: Psalms of Support and Encouragement (editor, 1995)
Finding Work without Losing Heart (1995)
The 365 Days of Christmas (1996)
Answers from Within (1998)
Jesuit Saturdays (2000)
A Book of Quiet Prayer (2006)
The Power of Principles (2006)

Table of Contents

Preface		ix
1	An Individuarian Outlook	1
2	The Beatitudes and Catholic Social Thought	7
3	An Attitude of Gratitude	17
4	Looking to the Year 2050	29
5	A Church in Crisis	45
6	Protecting Children from Pornography on the Internet	55
7	Organizational Ethics	61
8	Courage and Competence	77
9	Reasoned Argument about Abortion	89
10	Seeking Justice, Ending Hunger	95
11	Geno Baroni	103
12	Social Justice Education	113
13	Wealth and Responsibility	129
14	The Good Life	133
15	Workplace Spirituality	139
16	Spirituality and the Social Question	145

17	Religion and Politics	151
18	Becoming Ever More Human	155
19	Styles of Social Involvement	167
20	An Agenda for a Just Society	177
Origins and Acknowledgments		193
References		197
Index		201
About the Author		209

Preface

This book originated in an informal, no-fee, noncredit, adult education seminar at the University of Scranton in the winter of 2006. During my years as president there (1975–82), I made many friends in the Scranton community. One of them, Attorney Morey Myers, maintained close contact over subsequent years, so it was no surprise to get a call from him in the fall of 2005. It was, however, a bit of a surprise to learn that he, along with a local physician, and a professor of philosophy at the University, was planning a seminar on "The Individual and Society" for long-out-of-school professionals and others in the community, and that they would like to have me participate by delivering three lectures.

My immediate (but unexpressed) thought was about the risk of driving through the Baltimore-to-Scranton snow belt in February and March, so in accepting the invitation, I made provision for at least one cancellation due to icy, if not impassable, highways. As for the program, Morey, who had taken the group through the *Federalist Papers* the year before, would cover privacy and human rights issues in the law. Philosopher (and university provost) Hal Baillie would provide not only meeting space on campus but three lectures that would reach back to Plato and Aristotle up through John Locke and into contemporary philosophical reflection on the human person. My job would be to cover less theoretical terrain that would be broad enough to include the tradition of Catholic social thought and some practical social justice considerations deserving of discussion and debate in 2006. The physician, Harmar Brereton, an oncologist at Scranton's Mercy Hospital, would promote the seminar and be on hand to ask good questions and cheer us on.

As the opening paragraphs in chapters one and twenty will explain, those two chapters frame the contents of this book. They are linked directly to the seminar. They bookend the other chapters, so to speak, because instead of attempting to develop the individuarian theme into a full book (as University of Scranton Press director Jeff Gainey suggested might be desirable), I opted for the near-term possible over the longer-term desirable and searched my files for suitable material that would faithfully, if not comprehensively, represent Catholic social thought.

I dedicate this set of essays to Morey Myers and his wife Sondra, longtime friends of mine and both past trustees and loyal supporters of the University of Scranton. They have indeed made many good things happen in the Scranton community and far beyond.

WJB
Loyola College in Maryland
Summer, 2006

1

An Individuarian Outlook

I've often made the assertion, in print and speech, that there is no room for individualism in Catholic social teaching. But I was challenged on that point during a seminar on "The Individual and Society," a no-fee, noncredit, adult education course that attracted about thirty active and retired professionals and community-minded participants to a conference room at the University of Scranton on nine successive Thursday evenings (I was there for three) during the winter of 2006. At least one of the participants, a Jew, thought there should be a place for individualism in Catholic social thought and wondered aloud why I hadn't made room for it during my presentation on the principle of human dignity.

I explained that any *-ism* throws a noun into italics, so to speak, or gives it a boldface emphasis that almost always results in an imbalance. *Racism, sexism,* and *materialism* are just three examples I offered to make that point. I indicated that the word I've come up with to describe the individual who is autonomous and socially responsible is *individuarian.* The word is not in the dictionary, I acknowledged, but it is one I employ to describe persons who are neither rugged individualists nor ideological communists, even though they are strong-minded individuals.

I'm virtually certain that the term is original with me, although one can never be sure. To the best of my knowledge, I never heard it or saw it before in print. In any case, I employed it in my (2000) book *Jesuit Saturdays* to describe fairly and accurately, I thought, a somewhat common Jesuit personality type that I had observed over the years.

Although Jesuits live in community, *communism* would be an inappropriate label for Jesuit life. And individualism is not a characteristic that fairly describes the Jesuit spirit and spirituality. The typical Jesuit simply does not fit into this description of an individualist offered by Mary Douglas and Steven Ney: "Individualists, as the name implies, are not trying to create a community but rather aiming to free themselves from the fetters of social restriction. They thrive in loose organizational structures, around which they can move freely without long-term commitment, able to negotiate their own dealings with other individuals. Well-being for them means the freedom to pursue self-interested ends. It is the well-being of the narrowly defined ego, the ideal of negative freedom from interference" (1998, 122).

I'm not suggesting that no Jesuit ever fit or came close to fitting that description; I'm simply saying that most Jesuits have higher ideals, larger hearts, and wider horizons.

Just as *communitarian* is a label that came into currency some time ago to describe a socially responsible, environmentally sensitive, resourceful and self-starting citizen, *individuarian* comes to my mind now as a useful, even necessary label to describe the innovators and enablers we need to offset the community-eroding effects of individualism in our world today. You'll find them, although perhaps not enough of them, in all walks of life. They are the persons who, in my view, should be asserting themselves now if America is to find a balanced future somewhere between the extremes of individualism and what David Riesman many years ago called *groupism*.

The question raised in my first session in the Scranton seminar prompted me to reread (and later distribute to the seminar participants) a famous essay written by Riesman (1954) titled "Individualism Reconsidered." The meaning of individualism, he said, depends on the historical setting. In America at mid-twentieth century, he saw newer varieties of what he labeled "groupism" becoming "increasingly menacing," while there was a corresponding rise in a character orientation that he called "inner-direction" that was guided by values and ideals that made those who held them "appear to be more individualistic than they actually were." Note well the *appear to be* qualification that Riesman made.

To the extent that "capitalistic individualism has fostered an ethic of callousness," wrote Riesman decades before Enron, "the result has been to undermine all forms of individualism, good and bad."

So I've come up with *individuarian* to describe a good form of individualism. It is needed now to protect the common good from the extremes of self-centeredness on the one hand or mindless groupism on the other.

How then do I elucidate the meaning of this term? What other words describe the values and qualities of a genuine individuarian? Notice, by the way, that, like individuarian, each embodies an internal "r." *Responsibility* would be one such word; *trust*, *transparency*, *solidarity*, and *respect* would be others. Toward the top of the list I would put *character*, *courage*, and *integrity*. *Veracity*, *fairness*, *participation*, *generosity*, *charity*, and *humanitarian* bring additional dimensions to a category that serves to classify the strong individual who is intent on contributing to a stronger and measurably more just society by protecting and advancing the common good.

INDIVIDUAL CATALYSTS FOR CHANGE

Society, through its families, schools, faith communities, voluntary organizations, and corporations, has to begin cultivating this personality type now, if society hopes to enlist such persons in what strikes me as a long-deferred societal self-improvement campaign. Although I'll be restricting my examples to the United States, there are no national boundaries that limit the potential supply of individual catalysts for change that I choose to call individuarians.

Several books published shortly before the 2006 Scranton seminar spotlight three interesting individuarians—Abraham Lincoln, Milton S. Hershey, and Martin Luther King.

Doris Kearns Goodwin's (2005) *Team of Rivals: The Political Genius of Abraham Lincoln* ends with Leo Tolstoy's question, "Why was Lincoln so great that he overshadows all of the national heroes?" Tolstoy's answer: "His supremacy expresses itself altogether in his peculiar moral power and his greatness of character.... Lincoln was a humanitarian as broad as the world." Nice bridge, I would say, between the individual and the common good, which, for Lincoln, were the preservation of the Union and the restoration of freedom and dignity to enslaved human beings.

I expected Michael D'Antonio's (2006) *Hershey: Milton S. Hershey's Extraordinary Life of Wealth, Empire, and Utopian Dream* to deliver a portrait of the quintessential individualist. But D'Antonio states, "If it's a rule that behind every great fortune lies a great crime, M.S. Hershey was the exception."

Hershey was by no means perfect, but D'Antonio finds truth in the "florid terms" a local newspaper used in describing him in 1912, as "one man, inspired with acute foresight and shrewd business acumen, combined with a sense of justice—rare combination!—and recognizing the tremendous value of cooperation, raised a monument to himself by elevating the conditions of others." The monument was indeed "to himself," but it provided a town (planned but not patriarchal), a chocolate company that employed thousands (not without labor disputes), and a free school for disadvantaged children (two thousand now enrolled) that is better endowed than all but a handful of universities. "He was the good millionaire," writes D'Antonio. I would call Hershey an individuarian.

At Canaan's Edge, is volume three in Taylor Branch's (2006) masterful series, *America in the King Years*. "Like America's original Founders," writes Branch on the last page of this book, "those who marched for civil rights reduced power to human scale. They invested enormous hope in the capacity of ordinary people to create bonds of citizenship based on simple ideals... and in a sturdy design to balance self-government with public trust." King's oratory "mined twin doctrines of equal souls and equal votes in the common ground of nonviolence.... To the end, he resisted incitements to violence, cynicism, and tribal retreat." Not surprisingly, I would label Martin Luther King an individuarian.

Grateful as we are for these giants of the past, it is now time to look to emerging individuarians who can move the nation toward a better future. The 2006 Winter Olympics in Turin produced one—Joey Cheek, who donated his speed-skating prize money (a total of $40,000) to a charity that helps disadvantaged children through sports. Then there is Cindy Sheehan, who has truth to speak to power as she mourns the death of her soldier son in Iraq. Congressman Jack Murtha (Democrat of Pennsylvania), moved by his weekly visits to wounded service men and women flown back from Iraq to Walter Reed Hospital in Washington, DC, managed to get his Congressional friends and foes alike thinking seriously about planned withdrawal. Xerox CEO Anne Mulchay has restored tone at the top of a near-bankrupt corporate giant and is now guiding it to prosperity while offering example and encouragement to female aspirants to positions of leadership in business. These and many others are, in my view, emerging individuarians.

Readers of Thomas Friedman's (2005) *The World Is Flat* know that the empowerment of individuals to act on a global stage is the most important new feature of "the latest phase of globalization—the software revolution that enables an individual anywhere to become a player everywhere." It will be important, in my view, for these players to be genuine individuarians.

COOPERATION OVER COMPETITION

One way of encouraging the emergence of individuarians is to discourage toleration of conflicts of interest. Most energetic and talented individuals will have dualities of interest. Their jobs, ambitions, and community-mindedness will have them engaged with numerous organizations whose interests may at times intersect. If, at that juncture, self-enrichment, self-aggrandizement, and other selfish interests are permitted to trump the common good, the conflict is real and the interest of the community is injured. If, on the other hand, the potential conflict points to a community need that can be met by cooperation and a longer-term outlook, sensitive individuals can choose to become individuarians and make their respective contributions to a better community.

If motorists are more individuarian than individualist (e.g., car pooling, reducing speed, and riding a bike or the bus—instead of driving solo, speeding, and never considering alternative transportation), energy will be conserved. Similarly, to the extent that architects, builders, farmers, ranchers, miners, and manufacturers self-identify as individuarians instead of enclosing themselves in short-term, self-absorbed pursuits, the environment will be better served. As inventor or innovator, entrepreneur or manager, an individuarian will create employment and thus do good for others while doing well for him- or herself. Not to mention the contribution married individuarians will always make to the stability of marriage and family life.

Although respectful of competition and fully capable of confrontation, the individuarian prefers cooperation as an instrument of change on the way to community improvement. To the extent that it is possible to monitor a nation's *per-capita human impact*—what Jared Diamond calls "the average resource consumption and waste production of one person"—it becomes easier to see our need for individuarians. They're the ones who, while scaling back on resources consumed and waste produced, lift the disadvantaged and enlarge the common good, thus enhancing the possibility of a fuller share in the development of human potential for all of us. Diamond's most recent book (2005) is titled *Collapse: How Societies Choose to Fail or Succeed*. The subtitle suggests that although none of us can predict the future, we can—if only we can get ourselves together to talk about it—choose to have a better future. Individuarians can provide the imaginative leadership needed now to produce the wiser choices on which all else depends.

Jesuits, as I indicated earlier, tend to be individuarians. That, in my view, is one reason why they decided some years ago to set a goal for themselves in their schools and colleges of educating "men and women for others." Now *there* is another good way of describing an individuarian! And, in my view, an individuarian outlook is a good way to characterize what happens when one internalizes the principles of Catholic social teaching.

2

■

The Beatitudes and Catholic Social Thought

In the fifth chapter of Matthew's Gospel, you will find this account of Jesus teaching a concise summary of what it means to be a Christian, even though at that point in history there were no Christians, nor was there a Catholic Church. But the following set of ideas, intended to both describe and define Catholic Christians, was there for all within the range of the voice of Christ to consider those many centuries ago.

> When he saw the crowds, he went up the mountain, and after he had sat down, his disciples came to him. He began to teach them, saying: Blessed are the poor in spirit, for theirs is the kingdom of heaven. Blessed are they who mourn, for they will be comforted. Blessed are the meek, for they will inherit the land. Blessed are they who hunger and thirst for righteousness, for they will be satisfied. Blessed are the merciful, for they will be shown mercy. Blessed are the clean of heart, for they will see God. Blessed are the peacemakers, for they will be called children of God. Blessed are they who are persecuted for the sake of righteousness, for theirs is the kingdom of heaven. Blessed are you when they insult you and persecute you and utter every kind of evil against you (falsely) because of me. Rejoice and be glad, for your reward will be great in heaven. Thus they persecuted the prophets who were before you (Matt. 5:1–12).

These are the so-called *Beatitudes*—happiness qualities, blessings—although it takes a lot of faith to see the happiness there, to welcome them as blessings in your life. There are eight categories: the poor in spirit, those who mourn, the meek, those who hunger and thirst for justice, the merciful, the single-hearted, the peacemakers, and the persecuted.

A somewhat different version—a bit shorter and even more counter-cultural than Matthew's list— appears in the sixth chapter of the Gospel of Luke. There you can read the following:

> And he came down with them and stood on a stretch of level ground. A great crowd of his disciples and a large number of the people from all Judea and Jerusalem and the coastal region of Tyre and Sidon came to hear him and to be healed of their diseases; and even those who were tormented by unclean spirits were cured.
>
> Everyone in the crowd sought to touch him because power came forth from him and healed them all.
>
> And raising his eyes toward his disciples he said: "Blessed are you who are poor, for the kingdom of God is yours.
>
> "Blessed are you who are now hungry, for you will be satisfied. Blessed are you who are now weeping, for you will laugh.
>
> "Blessed are you when people hate you, and when they exclude and insult you, and denounce your name as evil on account of the Son of Man.
>
> "Rejoice and leap for joy on that day! Behold, your reward will be great in heaven. For their ancestors treated the prophets in the same way" (Luke 6:17–26).

The words that emerge here speak simply and starkly of the poor, the hungry, the weeping, the hated, excluded, and insulted. Note that Luke says poor, not poor in spirit.

During the 2004 presidential election campaign in the United States, there was a lot of discussion about how Catholics should vote and how presidential candidates and other office seekers matched up against Catholic teaching, values, principles, and ideals. My suggestion was then (and still is) to hold up the candidates and their party platforms against the background of the Beatitudes in order to see how well they matched up. There is no perfect match, of course, but this doesn't mean that the exercise is futile. It serves to remind us that the core message of Christianity is summarized in the Beatitudes. It also encourages a second look (or a see-it-again-for-the-first-time look) at the principles of Catholic social teaching, a body of doctrine that relates to issues raised in the Beatitudes.

Let me begin making this connection by remarking that principles, once internalized, lead to something. They prompt activity, impel motion, direct choices. A principled person always has a place to stand, knows where he or she is coming from and is likely to end up. Principles always lead the person who possesses them somewhere, for some purpose, to do something, or to choose not to.

AN ESSENTIAL PART OF THE CATHOLIC FAITH

In 1998, the NCCB (National Conference of Catholic Bishops, now the United States Conference of Catholic Bishops—USCCB) issued *Sharing Catholic Social Teaching: Challenges and Directions—Reflections of the U.S. Catholic Bishops*. With this document, they intended to call the attention of all U.S. Catholics to the existence of Catholic social principles—a body of doctrine with which, the bishops say, "far too many Catholics are not familiar." In fact, they add, "many Catholics do not adequately understand that the social teaching of the Church is an essential part of Catholic faith." Strong words.

A companion document, "Summary Report of the Task Force on Catholic Social Teaching and Catholic Education," is included in the same booklet that contains the bishops' reflections on this "serious challenge for all Catholics." I, along with about thirty others—educators from all levels, scholars, publishers, and social ministry professionals—served on the task force that produced the report.

The task force was convened in 1995 by the late Archbishop John R. Roach, then retired Archbishop of St. Paul and Minneapolis. Often during our periodic meetings over the course of two years, it occurred to me that one (admittedly only one) reason why the body of Catholic social teaching is under-appreciated, under-communicated, and not sufficiently understood is that the principles on which the doctrine is based are not clearly articulated and conveniently condensed. They are not "packaged" for catechetical purposes like the Ten Commandments and the seven sacraments. While many Catholics can come up with the eight Beatitudes and some would be willing to take a stab at listing the four cardinal virtues, few, if any, have a ready reply to the catechetical question the bishops want to raise: What are those Catholic social principles that are to be accepted as an essential part of the faith? The follow-up question, of course, asks how they can best be personally appropriated—internalized—so that they can lead to action.

On the tenth anniversary of their 1986 pastoral letter "Economic Justice for All," the bishops issued a ten-point summary of their teaching on the applicability of Catholic social principles to the economy. We on the task force had that summary in mind as we considered the broader issue of the applicability of Catholic social thought to a range of issues that go beyond the economic to include family, religious, social, political, technological, recreational, and cultural considerations. It would be a mistake, of course, to confine Catholic social teaching to the economic sphere.

How many Catholic social principles are there? Combing through the documents mentioned above, I have come up with ten. They are not listed by number in these documents. In one instance, I have split a single theme, articulated by the bishops, into two principles. There is nothing at all official about my count. Some future *Catechism of the Catholic Church* may list more or fewer than these ten, if compilers of that future teaching aid find that Catholic social teaching is suitable for framing in such a fashion. In any case, I offer my list of ten for three reasons: some reasonably complete list is needed if the ignorance cited by the bishops is going to be addressed; any list can serve to invite the hand of both editors and teachers to smooth out the sentences for clarity and ease of memorization; and any widely circulated list will stimulate further thought on the part of scholars and activists as to what belongs in a set of principles that can serve as a table of contents for the larger body of Catholic social teaching.

So, using these documents as my source, I here present ten principles of Catholic social teaching, which should not be seen as a rewriting of the documents, but simply as editing and reformatting.

1. The Principle of Human Dignity. "Every human being is created in the image of God and redeemed by Jesus Christ, and therefore is invaluable and worthy of respect as a member of the human family" (p.1). This is the bedrock principle of Catholic social teaching. Every person—regardless of race, sex, age, national origin, religion, sexual orientation, employment or economic status, health, intelligence, achievement, or any other differentiating characteristic—is worthy of respect. It is not what you do or what you have that gives you a claim on respect; it is simply *being* human that establishes your dignity. Given that dignity, the human person is, in the Catholic view, never a means, always an end.

The body of Catholic social teaching opens with the human person, but it does not close there. Individuals have dignity; individualism, understood as rugged individualism, has no place in Catholic social thought. The principle of human dignity gives the human person a claim on membership in a community, the human family.

2. The Principle of Respect for Human Life. "Every person, from the moment of conception to natural death, has inherent dignity and a right to life consistent with that dignity" (pp. 1–2). Human life at every stage of development and decline is precious and therefore worthy of protection and respect. It is always wrong directly to attack innocent human life. The Catholic tradition sees the sacredness of human life as part of any moral vision for a just and good society.

3. The Principle of Association. "Our tradition proclaims that the person is not only sacred but also social. How we organize our society—in economics and politics, in law and policy—directly affects human dignity and the capacity of individuals to grow in community" (p. 4). The centerpiece of society is the family; family stability must always be protected and never undermined. By association with others—in families and in other social institutions that foster growth, protect dignity, and promote the common good—human persons achieve their fulfillment.

4. The Principle of Participation. "We believe people have a right and a duty to participate in society, seeking together the common good and well-being of all, especially the poor and vulnerable" (p. 5). Without participation, the benefits available to an individual through any social institution cannot be realized. The human person has a right not to be shut out from participating in those institutions that are necessary for human fulfillment.

This principle applies in a special way to conditions associated with work. "Work is more than a way to make a living; it is a form of continuing participation in God's creation. If the dignity of work is to be protected, then the basic rights of workers must be respected—the right to productive work, to decent and fair wages, to organize and join unions, to private property, and to economic initiative" (p. 5).

5. The Principle of Preferential Protection for the Poor and Vulnerable. "In a society marred by deepening divisions between rich and poor, our tradition recalls the story of the last judgment (Matt. 25:31–46) and instructs us to put the needs of the poor and vulnerable first" (p. 5). Why is this so? Because the common good—the good of society as a whole—requires it. The opposite of rich and powerful is poor and powerless. If the good of all, the common good, is to prevail, preferential protection must move toward those affected adversely by the absence of power and the presence of privation. Otherwise the balance needed to keep society in one piece will be broken to the detriment of the whole.

6. The Principle of Solidarity. "Catholic social teaching proclaims that we are our brothers' and sisters' keepers, wherever they live. We are one human family.... Learning to practice the virtue of solidarity means learning that 'loving our neighbor' has global dimensions in an interdependent world" (p. 5). The principle of solidarity functions as a moral category that leads to choices that will promote and protect the common good.

7. The Principle of Stewardship. "The Catholic tradition insists that we show our respect for the Creator by our stewardship of creation" (p. 6). The steward is a manager, not an owner. In an era of rising consciousness about our physical environment, our tradition is calling us to a sense of moral responsibility for the protection of the environment—croplands, grasslands, woodlands, air, water, minerals, and other natural resources. Stewardship responsibilities also look toward our use of our personal talents, our attention to personal health, and our use of personal property.

8. The Principle of Subsidiarity. This principle deals chiefly with "the responsibilities and limits of government, and the essential roles of voluntary associations" (p. 6). The principle of subsidiarity puts a proper limit on government by insisting that no higher level of organization should perform any function that can be handled efficiently and effectively at a lower level of organization by human persons who, individually or in groups, are closer to the problems and closer to the ground. Oppressive governments are always in violation of the principle of subsidiarity; overactive governments frequently violate this principle.

All eight of these principles were culled from the relatively brief *Reflections of the U.S. Catholic Bishops*—as the second subtitle of *Sharing Catholic Social Teaching* describes this document of the NCCB. As I read on through the summary of the task force report, I found an articulation of two additional principles, which follow.

9. The Principle of Human Equality. "Equality of all persons comes from their essential dignity.... While differences in talents are a part of God's plan, social and cultural discrimination in fundamental rights...are not compatible with God's design" (pp. 23–24).

Treating equals equally is one way of defining justice, also understood classically as rendering to each person his or her due. Underlying the notion of equality is the simple principle of fairness; one of the earliest ethical stirrings felt in the developing human person is a sense of what is fair and what is not.

10. The Principle of the Common Good. "The common good is understood as the social conditions that allow people to reach their full human potential and to realize their human dignity" (p. 25). The social conditions the bishops have in mind presuppose respect for the person, the social well-being and development of the group, and the maintenance by public authority of peace and security. Today, "in an age of global interdependence," the principle of the common good points to the "need for international structures that can promote the just development of the human family across regional and national lines."

What constitutes the common good is always going to be a matter for debate. The absence of any concern for or sensitivity to the common good is a sure sign of a society in need of help. As a sense of community is eroded, concern for the common good declines. A proper communitarian concern is the antidote to unbridled individualism, which, like unrestrained selfishness in personal relations, can destroy balance, harmony, and peace within and among groups, neighborhoods, regions, and nations.

It would not be inconsistent with either the *Reflections* or the *Summary* to articulate a separate principle of justice and another principle that affirms both the right to private property and what the *Summary* calls the "universal destination of goods," by which is meant that the goods of this world are intended by God for the benefit of everyone. But these principles are implied in those already listed; so I'll stop counting at ten. The door remains wide open for additional themes, theses, or what I have been calling simply *principles*.

I am often asked what the difference is between a value and a principle. The terms are frequently used interchangeably. I like the leads-to-something implication of principle, while acknowledging that values, once internalized, will prompt people to act consistently with what they cherish and consider to be valuable—i.e., with what they judge to be worth their time, treasure, and talent. Neither principles nor values lead anywhere if they remain abstract, embalmed in print, or are not internalized by human persons and carried in human hearts. Encouraging internalization of these principles is a pedagogical challenge that could be the subject of another essay.

CREDENDA-AGENDA

By including Catholic social teaching among the essentials of the faith, the bishops are affirming the existence of *credenda* (things to be believed) that become, in the believer, a basis for the *agenda* (things to be done) the believer must follow. Thus Catholic social action flows from Catholic social doctrine. How to bring the social portion of the doctrine of the faith to the attention of believers is the challenge the bishops have now put once again before Catholic pastors and educators at every level.

By the arrangement I've attempted here, this agenda rests on ten building blocks:

Human Person	Solidarity	Preference for the Poor
Human Life	Stewardship	Common Good
Association	Subsidiarity	
Participation	Equality	

People who enjoy coming up with acronyms could rearrange the order to construct an easily remembered set of capital letters. Whatever the order and regardless of the labels, this set of principles might constitute topics for an adult education lecture series, segments for a semester-long course, chapters in a textbook, offices or sections in a research center or simply ten "bins" for gathering the collected wisdom drawn from Scripture; patristic literature; Scholastic, conciliar, and papal teaching; church history; systematic, moral, and pastoral theology; and the ever-developing body of social reflection coming from episcopal conferences and other sources.

Not to be overlooked is the possibility of ten biographical essays focusing on persons who embodied one or more of these principles in a significant way—Dorothy Day, Cardinal Joseph Bernardin, and Mother Teresa, for instance. Also possible would be a collection of excerpts, organized under these ten headings, from Chrysostom, Ambrose, Aquinas, and other great social voices from the Catholic past. If they are to be taught, the principles need a human face; the lessons have to be conveyed in words and images that move the heart.

These ten organizational categories can accommodate every conceivable social issue; they can provide any social problem with an analytical home. Analysis and reflection targeted on this material can become the base for moral instruction and formation of conscience. And that, of course, is the whole point of bringing Catholic education and Catholic social teaching together into the new working partnership hoped for by the National Conference of Catholic Bishops. Meanwhile, the interested inquirer can find references for further reading in the back of the NCCB booklet, or one could simply consult the index in the new (1992) *Catechism of the Catholic Church* for leads to fuller explanations of Catholic social teaching. And if anyone wonders why the Catholic bishops reflect and write occasionally about war, peace, nuclear weapons, the economy, abortion, euthanasia, health insurance, and a wide range of other topics that have a clear social and moral dimension, these principles provide the necessary interpretive framework for understanding the significance of the bishops' pastoral letters. They cannot be dismissed out of hand as political tracts; they must be held in respect as important instruments for teaching the Catholic faith.

3

■

An Attitude of Gratitude

A midwinter 2006 phone call from a veteran pastor started me thinking about a springtime solution to a set of problems just beginning to surface in a vibrant suburban parish in the East. I won't name the diocese or the parish, because the emerging problems would not fairly characterize the parish community. Most of his parishioners were unaware of the pastor's concerns.

He saw troubling signs of class distinction emerging in his parish. A low-income youngster was withdrawn by his parents from the parish school because other children made fun of him for wearing inexpensive sneakers that were the wrong brand—not cool, not what the with-it (i.e., wealthier) kids were wearing. He was also troubled by the fact that at least one parishioner stopped coming to Mass because of the color of the skin of a substitute priest who celebrated daily and Sunday Masses for two weeks while the pastor was away on vacation. When he returned, he was confronted by the disgruntled parishioner who announced, in language strengthened by an offensive racial epithet, his decision to leave the parish.

There were also euphemistic references to "cultural considerations" by at least one other parishioner in a conversation about the use of parish resources to assist poor persons and minority groups.

Three isolated events. Three quiet signals. Not a widespread problem by any means, but a problem nonetheless. How to address it was the pastor's question to me.

We came up with the idea of a parishwide preparation for First Communion. I agreed to give two talks and provide suitable reading material. An announcement went out to the entire parish inviting adults to two successive Thursday-evening presentations toward the end of Lent. The children would be prepared in the parochial school or through weekend religious education, the notice said; the adults were invited to participate in what many might welcome as a theological "tune-up" to prepare themselves for a fuller parish celebration of First Eucharist. No mention was made of the issues that prompted the pastor's call to me.

I lifted from my (1976) files an article I wrote for *America*. It was published to coincide with the opening of the forty-first International Eucharistic Congress, which was held in that American Bicentennial Year in Philadelphia. The Congress theme was "The Hungers of the Human Family." I took that as a prompt to discuss the Eucharist as meal, presence, and sacrifice. Here, in summary, are highlights from the article, which was reproduced these many years later for distribution to participants in this parishwide preparation for First Communion.

My thesis was that when the accent of theological interest shifts from one aspect of the mystery of the Eucharist to another, there will be corresponding behavioral shifts in the worshipping community. For example, when the accent is on presence and the theologians offer explanations of how (not *if*, but *how*) Christ is really present under the appearance of bread and wine, the behavior patterns incorporate silence, distance, adoration, gold vessels, relatively rare reception, fasting before reception, and other practices that older Catholics remember well.

With the accent on Eucharist as sacrifice—on our belief that the unique sacrifice of Jesus on the Cross is made present again on our altars at every Mass—the crucifix is prominently displayed on or over the altar. It is a high altar at one end of a cruciform church. The celebrant has his back to the people who gather in relative isolation from one another, intent upon being "there when they crucified my Lord." It is a ritual of praise, adoration, reparation, and thanksgiving; the "fruits" of the Mass may be applied by intention of the celebrant and the people to the designated needs of the living and the dead.

EUCHARIST AS MEAL

With the Second Vatican Council (1962–65), the theological accent fell on Eucharist as meal. Worshippers could now gather, so to speak, around the table of the Lord because the altar was indeed turned around and the celebrant now faced the people, who joined him in praying the Mass in the vernacular.

A shift of theological reflection from one aspect of the mystery of the Eucharist to another in no way implies a denial or denigration of truths previously emphasized, even though there may be a devotional departure from previous practices. Moreover, worshippers whose devotional practices are rooted in another doctrinal emphasis—presence or sacrifice—may be uncomfortable in the more familial, even conversational, environment that is congenial with an emphasis on Eucharist as meal.

Some worshippers bristle at the thought of shaking another's hand, in the gesture known as the "kiss of peace," before reception of Communion. Indeed some prefer not to receive Communion in the hand as is recommended but not required in the post-Vatican II Church.

OPEN HANDS AND OPEN HEARTS

I mentioned to this parish audience that, on occasion, resistance is raised when I make the following catechetical point about preparation during Mass for reception of Holy Communion. Your posture of standing with open hands (or hands joined to the hands of those on either side) to recite the Our Father, followed by receiving the hand of another along with the prayerful expression that the "peace of Christ" may be yours and theirs, leads directly to the moment when you receive in your hand the body of Christ—body and blood, soul and divinity, as you firmly believe. If your hand and heart are closed to those around you (perhaps because of racial, ethnic, class, or other differences), and if the peace of Christ is not shared between you (because of prejudice, an unwillingness to forgive, or worse), you have to wonder about your worthiness to receive Holy Communion, and this realization can, understandably, come as a shock. With the emphasis on

Eucharist as meal, the liturgy encourages (really requires) the worshipper to look horizontally to those with whom he or she forms the one body of Christ, not just vertically to the risen Christ whose victory won for all the gift of salvation.

I pointed out to the parish audience that emphasis on Eucharist as meal is surely going to trigger a replay of the words that formed the title of a famous Sidney Poitier 1967 movie: "Guess Who's Coming to Dinner." In our parish celebration of Eucharist, is there room at the table for all of God's children? The question cannot be ignored.

I explored in the article, which, by the way, was titled "Eucharist and Society," and in these recent parish presentations, the relationship of social justice to the celebration of Eucharist. The "Hungers of the Human Family," highlighted in the Bicentennial Year, included our hunger for peace as well as for the bread for life. We still live today in a world broken by unshared bread, I reminded this parish audience. Eucharist should nourish our determination to heal that broken world. We might, I suggested (repeating a suggestion made by a speaker at the 1976 Congress), think about reviving the pre-Eucharistic fast in a new and creative way: whenever we share the bread of life, we should take steps to share the bread for life—i.e., the food the hungry need to stay alive.

THE IMPORTANCE OF ATTITUDE

As a lead-in to full disclosure about what the pastor and I were up to in offering these sessions on the Eucharist, I took the audience back forty-four years to a riveting moment in the history of this nation's space exploration program. I did it to highlight the importance and meaning of the word *attitude*.

I mentioned that some would remember February 20, 1962 when America's pioneer astronaut John Glenn blasted into orbit as part of the space race between the United States and the Soviet Union. We were behind in that race and John Glenn's success in orbiting the earth three times on that sunny day more than four decades ago did much to restore American prestige worldwide as well as advance our progress in space exploration.

Glenn's Mercury spacecraft was Friendship 7. In it, Marine Colonel Glenn risked his life as he traveled at 17,500 miles per hour 160 miles above Earth. His autopilot function failed and he had to pilot the spacecraft manually. The world watched on television and listened to Mission Control wonder aloud whether the space capsule's heat shield would hold while reentering the earth's atmosphere, because, as the spacecraft began its second orbit, Mission Control received a signal that the heat shield was loose. Its function was to prevent the capsule from burning up during reentry. Normally the retrorockets would be jettisoned after they were fired to slow the capsule for reentry. In this case, however, Glenn was ordered to retain them in order to hold the heat shield in place. As he struggled to maintain control of the spacecraft, Colonel Glenn watched as huge chunks flew past the window and he wondered whether it was the retropack or the heat shield breaking up. The world held its breath at reentry time. The heat shield held. If it hadn't, John Glenn and his capsule would have been incinerated.

During those tense moments of flight maneuvers and instruction, the word *attitude* was frequently used by Mission Control, referring to the attitude of the space craft. I was intrigued by that vocabulary and soon realized, of course, that they were talking about the tilt, the direction of incline, the bias, the position of the capsule. It had to be tilted so that the heat shield would be properly aligned, if indeed it was still attached to the spacecraft, to make first contact with the earth's atmosphere. It was there. It held. John Glenn lived to tell the story of the flight. History was made. The mission was a success.

"HE EMPTIED HIMSELF"

"Have in you the same attitude that is also in Christ Jesus," writes St. Paul in his Letter to the Philippians (2:5). He is inviting them and us, I suggested to this parish audience, to have a tilt, a bias, a direction, a mindset, an attitude. That tilt cannot be simply a nod or salute to Christ Jesus. More is required of the Christian than a membership card. There has to be commitment to the values of Jesus, a fidelity in following his way, a willingness to imitate him, to internalize his worldview, to adopt his convictions, to make them our own, to internalize them. In other words, with the controls of your own life in your own hands (manual control, no autopilot), you have to tilt your life as Jesus tilted his. And what was his tilt, his bias, his attitude? Paul outlines it this way: "Though he was in the form of God, [Jesus] did not regard equality with God something to be grasped. Rather, he emptied himself, taking the form of a slave coming in human likeness; and found human in appearance, he humbled himself, becoming obedient to the point of death, even death on a cross" (Phil. 2:6–8).

But Paul is quick to add: "Because of this, God greatly exalted him and bestowed on him the name that is above every other name."

He *emptied* himself. The Greek word for that is *kenosis* and the voluntary emptying out of power and glory on the part of Jesus in order to take our flesh and become like us so that he could save us, is sometimes called a "kenotic gesture." He didn't cling to his equality with God as a miser clings to his treasure. No; he let go; he emptied himself. "Found human in appearance, he humbled himself," says Paul of Jesus. We have to think of ourselves in those terms, I said, and then added: Are we sufficiently humble to live a poured-out life, as Jesus did? He valued humility. He committed himself to a personal emptying out. Where are our values? What are our commitments?

A NASA news release that I saw just a few years ago announced that something called the Global Positioning System is now "determining the attitude, position, and speed of the International Space Station." I shared that with the parishioners and then said that here on earth, as our feet of clay try to find their way on the journey of faith, the word of God, preserved for us in the books of the Bible, should function as a positioning system, an attitude setter. I said we might think of the Beatitudes, for example, in Matthew, and ask: Are we aligned with those values? Whether you imagine yourself to be in a space capsule or a canoe in your journey of faith, I said, you can slip off course. You can tilt in the wrong direction. You can find yourself on a sharp incline that can let you slide away from God. You can cultivate biases (or permit a secular culture to cultivate them for you) that run counter to the attitude that Jesus cultivated for himself and wants to share with you.

This selection from Philippians is just one of many readings that can be factored into a personal "positioning system." The entire Sermon on the Mount can work well toward that end. We should all be looking around for our own way of living the poured-out life, of emptying ourselves out for others. This is not doormat spirituality because the upside for us, as it was for Jesus, is also articulated by Paul in the same Philippians text: "Because of this, God greatly exalted him and bestowed on him the name which is above every name, that at the name of Jesus every knee should bend, of those in heaven and on earth and under the earth, and every tongue confess that Jesus Christ is Lord, to the glory of God the Father" (Phil. 2:9–11).

You can't expect that knees will bend before you, but you can bet your life on the glory that awaits you in Christ Jesus your Lord if you make his attitude your own. I reminded the parishioners that in our first session together I had remarked that since the earliest days of the Church, the Eucharist has been referred to as the "medicine of immortality." Take it and you will live forever!

FOCUS ON THE FURNITURE

In that same first session, I related that when I was a pastor at Holy Trinity in Washington, DC, I would gather together in the church all the children who were preparing for First Communion. I would ask them what they regarded as the most important place or piece of furniture there in the setting where the Eucharist is celebrated. We would acknowledge the importance of the tabernacle, the crucifix, the ambo from which the Word of God is proclaimed and explained, and the celebrant's chair, but we would agree that the central feature—the most important piece of furniture in the church—is the table. The turned-around table is an altar, to be sure, but not a high altar separated from the people. It is a gathering place intended for the sharing of a meal by those who remember their Lord in the breaking of the bread.

I would also point out to the youngsters (and I made the same point with this adult-parishioner audience) that there is never a children's table in church, as there often is in the family home at Thanksgiving and Christmas dinners. No children's table in church (even though there may be children's Masses) because you have to be big enough to believe a few things before you can take a place at the Table of the Lord. Recalling those *few things* is a good way of engaging a parish in preparation for First Communion.

All acknowledge that you have to believe that this is truly the body and blood, soul and divinity of Jesus Christ made present here on this table under the appearance of bread and wine—it just looks like bread and wine, we tell the children, tastes like bread and wine, but during Mass it becomes the body and blood of Christ. And you have to be big enough to believe that all who come to this table receive the identical portion, not a share of Christ's body and blood, but the same body and blood of Jesus that all other communicants receive. Unlike the ordinary food that we eat each day for nourishment and that becomes part of us, we explain to the children, this Eucharistic food works just the other way around—we become part of it. By participating in the Eucharist, we become divinized. And, of course, it takes time for all of us, not just the children, to grasp that truth.

To the extent that words from the liturgy aid the explanation, I point out that when the priest lets a drop of water fall into the chalice at the offertory, he prays: "By the mystery of this water and wine, may we share in the divinity of Christ who humbled himself to share in our humanity." If you pay attention to those words, you realize that he is saying that we become divinized. We are nourished, of course, but instead of the food becoming part of us, we become part of it. I recalled in the opening presentation that the familiar biblical story of the manna in the desert prefigured the Eucharist. The people gathered it up outside their tents each morning during the Exodus; it was their day's food for their day's march in exile. So I said that we receive Holy Communion as our day's food, or our weekly food, to nourish us in our journey of faith.

AN ATTITUDE OF GRATITUDE

In our opening session, I made a big point of the fact that Eucharist means thanksgiving, thanks-saying, thanks-doing. Our Sunday obligation is really to give praise and thanks to God for the gift of our redemption in and through the death and resurrection of Christ. We say thanks. Ritually, we do thanks. We declare ourselves to be "much obliged." I pointed out how important it is to recall that we as a worshipping, celebrating Sunday people are a grateful people. We should be constantly trying to develop in our hearts and minds an attitude of gratitude. At the root of all sinfulness is some form of ingratitude. And as I told the parishioners in our opening session, it is simply impossible for any human being to be simultaneously grateful and unhappy.

So it is in your immediate self-interest, I told this audience, that if you want to be happy (and I think it is safe to say that all of us want that), you should be attentive to your attitude of gratitude. And finally, I noted that Jesus chose for our sake to be like bread broken and passed around, like a cup poured out, and that he invites us who would call ourselves Christian to be exactly like that—to become bread broken for the nourishment of others, to be like cups poured out in service to others.

Well into the second session, mindful of the need for a "takeaway"—an enduring idea and practice—when our parish preparation program ended, I asked the parishioners, whose attention had been directed to the altar-table before them, to try to impress upon themselves the importance of an attitude of gratitude. This should coexist, I said, with a good Catholic's reverence and respect for the Eucharist. I then took them back to review a centuries-old problem concerning participation in the Eucharistic meal that St. Paul had to deal with in the Corinthian community. I asked them to listen to Paul addressing divisions within the Christian community at Corinth: "I urge you brothers [and sisters], in the name of our Lord Jesus Christ, that all of you agree in what you say, and that there be no divisions among you, but that you be united in the same mind and in the same purpose. For it has been reported to me about you, my brothers [and sisters]...that there are rivalries among you...." (1 Cor. 1:10–11). Suggesting that Paul was a pastor with some splits in his community that required attention, I asked them to keep listening. "Avoid idolatry. I am speaking as to sensible people; judge for yourselves what I am saying. The cup of blessing that we bless, is it not a participation in the blood of Christ? The bread that we break, is it not a participation in the body of Christ? Because the loaf of bread is one, we, though many, are one body, for we partake in the one loaf" (1 Cor. 10:14–17).

And citing an abuse at Corinth relative to the celebration of the Lord's Supper, Paul writes words that might have an application in our own times: "In giving this instruction, I do not praise the fact that our meetings [liturgies] are doing more harm than good. First of all, I hear that when you meet as a church there are divisions among you, and to a degree I believe it; there have to be factions among you in order that those who are approved among you may become known. When you meet in one place, then, it is not to eat the Lord's supper, for in eating, each one goes ahead with his own supper, and one goes hungry while another gets drunk. Do you not have houses in which you can eat and drink? Or do you show contempt for the church of God and make those who have nothing feel ashamed? What can I say to you? Shall I praise you? In this matter I do not praise you" (1 Cor. 11:17–22).

NO MORE FACTIONS

The "essence of Paul's reaction is that there can be no Eucharist in a community whose members do not love one another," writes Jerome Murphy-O'Connor, O.P. (1990, 809), in his commentary on 1 Corinthians in *The New Jerome Biblical Commentary*.

Paul's reference to making "those who have nothing feel ashamed" echoes the problem of the youngster with the wrong kind of sneakers withdrawing from the community of this modern parish. The statement that "there have to be factions among you in order that those who are approved among you may become known" would not have much application to these parishioners today simply because it refers to the fact that the meeting (Eucharistic meal) in Corinth was held in a private house with small rooms and the division imposed by the small rooms aggravated a situation caused by the Roman custom of separating guests by social class, with little or nothing going to those in the lower class—"... for in eating, each one goes ahead with his own supper, and one goes hungry while another gets drunk." Paul is saying that there is no Eucharist there. There are "factions among you in order that those who are approved among you may become better known. When you meet [in this way] it is not to eat the Lord's supper." There is no Eucharist there, says St. Paul. It is up to us to notice the possibility of modern parallels to this divided community situation in our own parishes today.

St. Paul gives the earliest account of the institution of the Eucharist in the New Testament:

> For I received from the Lord what I also handed on to you, that the Lord Jesus, on the night he was handed over, took bread, and, after he had given thanks, broke it and said, "This is my body that is for you. Do this in remembrance of me." In the same way also the cup, after supper, saying, "This cup is the new covenant in my blood. Do this, as often as you drink it, in remembrance of me." For as often as you eat this bread and drink this cup, you proclaim the death of the Lord until he comes. Therefore, whoever eats the bread or drinks the cup of the Lord unworthily will have to answer for the body and blood of the Lord. A person should examine himself, and so eat the bread and drink the cup. For anyone who eats and drinks without discerning the body, eats and drinks judgment on himself. That is why many among you are ill and infirm, and a considerable number are dying. [Remarkably, Paul is saying that widespread illness and death among them is a sign of divine punishment for their lack of love and their unworthy celebration of the Eucharist.] If we discerned ourselves, we would not be under judgment; but since we are judged by the Lord, we are being disciplined so that we may not be condemned along with the world.
>
> Therefore, my brothers [and sisters], when you come together to eat, wait for one another. If anyone is hungry, he should eat at home, so that your meetings [liturgies] may not result in judgment. The other matters [commentators say these other matters are minor liturgical abuses] I shall set in order when I come (1 Cor. 11:23–34).

It cannot be overemphasized that Paul is saying that the Eucharist is a source of union for Christians—union not only of the Christian with Christ, but union of Christians with one another. Hence division in a parish community along race, class, or cultural lines is incompatible with the celebration of the Eucharist.

I know a priest who adds a phrase to the payer all priests say when offering the wine: "Praise to you Lord God of all creation, through your goodness we have this wine to offer, fruit of the vine *and work of migrant labor*, let it become for us our spiritual drink." The obvious point, which surely grates on the ears of some, is that those Latino hands help to make our offering possible.

When this parish exercise began, I quoted the following paragraph from my *America* article that had been distributed, and I repeated it in the second lecture:

> In a certain sense, the contemporary Catholic community is risking just about everything it has when it speaks of Eucharist as meal and says that this sacrament can, in today's alienated and privatized social environment, effect what it signifies, namely, community. In other periods of our history, we have stressed the power the Eucharist has to unify the believer with God; we viewed Eucharist as a source of unity in that sense. Today, we also see Eucharist as a source of unity between believer and believer who, sharing the one loaf and the one cup, themselves become one. The many become a community in Christ. But will it happen in our time? Will this sacrament effect what it signifies? We must not be anxious abut the outcome, for the Eucharistic assembly is formed through faith. It is all God's work.

Indeed it is all God's work, but assisting in that work is our responsibility.

In meeting that responsibility, what can any one person do? I suggest that all of us should first cultivate an attitude of gratitude, and then keep the focus on the table. Designers, architects, and ordinary sanctuary furniture movers can make it easier for all of us to focus attention on the table. But it is up to each of us individually to foster within ourselves an attitude—a tilt, a bias, a predisposition—of gratitude. As that attitude spreads, evidence will emerge of happier, more welcoming congregations, quite literally embodying the love the Lord bequeathed to his Church.

4

Looking to the Year 2050

An invitation from the British Province of the Society of Jesus to speak to a Directors of Work Conference, in Oxford, England, November 5, 2004, gave me a great opportunity to do some forward thinking. Where would the Society of Jesus be in the year 2050? What would the Church look like at the middle of the twenty-first century? What might an American experience of church and change offer for consideration to like-minded Jesuits and their lay colleagues in the United Kingdom? What might the British experience have to contribute to the planning mix in North America?

My presentation was intended to serve as a discussion paper for the consideration of Jesuits and others interested in the question of Jesuit recruitment, and also for Jesuits and lay colleagues interested in the future of Jesuit works. By way of pre-note, I offered to the Oxford audience of Jesuits and lay colleagues a premise, a suggestion, a favorite quotation, and a verse from Scripture.

- **My premise:** You cannot predict the future but you can choose a future. At least you can choose some characteristics of the future you would like to have.
- **A suggestion:** In his history, *The First Jesuits*, John W. O'Malley, S.J. (1993, 72–73) points out that "one of the most striking features of the early Jesuits is the wide variety of people to whom they ministered, including many of the poor and outcast." He also cites Jerome Nadal as being insightful

on the Pauline characteristic of our ministry. Shortly after the death of Ignatius, Nadal wrote in his personal journal: "The Society has the care of those souls for whom either there is nobody to care or, if somebody ought to care, the care is negligent. This is its [the Society's] dignity in the Church." O'Malley says that for Nadal, "the Jesuit task par excellence was to search for the 'lost sheep'— whether pagan, Muslim, heretic, or Catholic." In summing up, O'Malley again quotes Nadal who wrote: "Paul signifies for us our ministry" (Ibid., 73).

- And so, my suggestion: Read St. Paul to discover clues to guide your reflection and choices about the substance and style of future Jesuit ministries.
- The quotation: "The Society of Jesus formally lives on its trust in each of its members. Each day in their life is a hundredfold appeal to their independence and energetic sense of duty, to their free good will, to their high-hearted love of Christ." (Peter Lippert, S.J., who entered the German Province in 1899, worked as a writer and radio commentator, was a frequent contributor to *Stimmen der Zeit* and author of several books; he died at age 57 in 1937. John Courtney Murray, S.J. used the Lippert quotation in Murray's address given on the occasion of the seventy-fifth anniversary of Woodstock College in 1944.)
- A Scripture reading from Deuteronomy (30:19–20): "I have set before you life and death, the blessing and the curse. Choose life, then, that you and your descendants may live, by loving the Lord, your God, heeding his voice, and holding fast to him." (This familiar "choose life" text is part of the first reading for the Mass of St. Ignatius Loyola on July 31.)

In our collective desire to choose life, I told the Oxford audience, I think we have to begin with some assumptions about the Church in the year 2050. What might the Church be like at the midpoint of this century? We then should attempt to identify some elements of competence that will be needed to serve that Church (competencies that are therefore desirable, at least in potential, in candidates now entering the Society of Jesus).

As I opened this up, I acknowledged my own incompetence to identify and interpret the signs of these times in Great Britain with any precision. Later in the presentation, I would speak along parallel lines to reflections on the signs I see in the United States.

I offered, as one man's opinion, a description of what Jesuit commitment might look like in the future we can hope for, and listed some strategic conclusions relating to promoting vocations and the recruitment of Jesuits in the United States, while opening the door to reflections on Jesuit recruitment in the United Kingdom.

My opening emphasis on Jesuit recruitment is not at all an indication of disinterest in the recruitment of lay colleagues for Jesuit works, nor would I want to exclude lay voices from this conversation about the recruitment of Jesuits. Quite the contrary. The point, however, that I hoped to emphasize is that we do want more Jesuits—more bright, holy, generous young men, to enter the Society and to be there with the lay colleagues we also hope to attract to commit themselves to Jesuit works.

We know we have to be careful with respect to what we pray for, and ready to work to get that for which we pray. So discernment—personal, community-wide, province-wide, and even wider—is necessary if we are to both pray and work for what God wants to send our way in response to our prayers and efforts for vocations to the Society of Jesus.

ASSUMPTIONS

I numbered the following assumptions for easy identification and to encourage additions, subtractions, substitutions, and deletions as others articulate their own assumptions about what the community we call the Church is likely to become over the next fifty years. My focus was primarily on the Catholic Church USA, distinct but not apart from the Church universal. But I acknowledged that international-mindedness will be a characteristic of American Jesuits and that service in other countries and cultures will be expected of them. And I invited all to think, as I moved down this list, of the alternate or additional assumptions others would regard as appropriate for our conversation about the Jesuit future in the United Kingdom.

1. Lay presence and influence will continue to grow in the institutional life of the Catholic Church USA.
2. The clerical culture will diminish but not disappear; the episcopal component of that culture will continue to display an inability to differentiate influence from control. (American bishops tend to believe that in order to have more influence, they have to have more control).
3. The promotion culture within the hierarchical structure of the Church will persist and thus continue to foster ambition, which, if not moderated by a spirituality of servant leadership, will continue to be corrosive within the Catholic community.
4. Optional celibacy for diocesan priests will become part of Catholic life within two decades, thus easing what is perceived to be an imminent priest shortage.
5. Women will continue their rise in positions of responsibility and influence in the institutional Church and could perhaps find ordination an option open to them by the year 2050. If women are ordained, there will be no priest shortage in the United States.
6. Catholic participation in interfaith marriages will continue to increase.
7. Religious literacy among Catholics will continue to decline.
8. The Catholic population will continue to increase in America—more by immigration than by conversion or birth into Catholic families.
9. Educational attainment and family income of American Catholics will, on average, continue to rise, but family size will not.
10. Catholic representation in positions of political and business leadership will increase.
11. Catholic education at all levels—primary, secondary, and higher education—will remain strong but enroll a relatively small portion of the Catholic population in those three student-age groups.

12. Catholic representation in positions of intellectual leadership, although not insignificant, will be less than proportional to their numbers in the general population.
13. Catholic influence in literature and the arts will not be particularly strong.
14. The influence of Catholic moral theology on sexual behavior, and medical and life-science experimentation will not be great.
15. In the context of a widening gap between rich and poor in the world, Catholics in the United States will not differ significantly from other Americans in their concern for social justice.

Many more assumptions can be listed. Jesuits and lay colleagues acknowledge (and respect) the fact that each person is the world's leading expert on his or her own opinion. Different opinions will generate additional assumptions, which, in turn, will contribute to the production of better conclusions about preparation for and delivery of Jesuit service to the Church in the year 2050. To offset the possible misperception that all this is too narrowly American, I repeated that I'm assuming an international-mindedness in Jesuit recruits and I wanted the British directors to state the assumptions that apply best to the Church in the United Kingdom.

COMPETENCIES

Here, in my view, are the talents and skills that Jesuits will need in order to be effective ministers to the Catholic Church USA in 2050. I realize that the Lord has a penchant for writing straight with crooked lines and uses the lowly to confound the proud. I know that the distribution of talents, in God's gracious providence, is uneven, and I certainly acknowledge that calling men to the Society is God's work that will be done in God's wise ways (with a wisdom that is not of this world). But there is no reason for us not to try to attract (not simply hope for, but attract) the very best talent to our ranks.

I'm convinced that anyone whom God calls to Jesuit life can become very good in the exercise of at least one ministerial skill. I should make clear that I am not ignoring in this consideration the vocation of the Jesuit brother, those who are not called to Holy Orders but are called to be vowed religious in the Society of Jesus. Brothers will have ministerial opportunities in the future that they did not have in the past; they will also have opportunities to excel in practical, secular pursuits related to the Society's changing mission to a world in need of help. Nor, to repeat, am I unmindful of the need to attract non-Jesuits to Jesuit works if those works are to survive, much less prosper, in 2050. With that said, let me suggest that candidates for admission to the Society now should have the following: (1) the potential to become competent, even outstanding schoolmasters, professors, scholars, pastors, and preachers; (2) the potential to develop skills for teaching, preaching, researching, speaking (in more than one language), writing, listening, community organizing, and giving spiritual direction; (3) the potential to become expert in spiritual discernment and the personal assimilation and apostolic application of the Spiritual Exercises; and (4) the demonstrated ability to live and work well with others.

These competencies are rather general; within each category there is need for early assimilation of skills and, with the benefit of coaching and practice, the perfection of these skills to a high level.

I asked the audience to hold my feet to the small fire I ignited with my opening suggestion about St. Paul being a model for Jesuit ministries. You will recall the words of Nadal: "Paul signifies for us our ministry." Keep that in mind in considering all that follows.

COMMITMENT

Commitment is a characteristic that every Jesuit must have. I would expect a candidate for entrance into the Society to be committed: (1) to celibacy: (2) to locating himself personally within the Paschal Mystery—i.e., to living "under the banner of the Cross" with the certain hope of participation in the Easter victory, and therefore living as a man of hope; (3) to serving the Holy See through obedience to superiors in the Society, and with this, being committed to working anywhere in the world for the greater glory of God; (4) to helping others (our founding documents said, "helping souls," and we would now say, "being men for others"); and (5) to Christ (it goes without saying—although Peter Lippert said it well—that there is an ongoing commitment to Christ, a "high-hearted love of Christ").

STRATEGIC CONCLUSIONS

Now to bring this down to the level of practical choice and strategic planning, I point out first that strategic planning begins with strategic thinking, and strategic thinking has to begin with a question. *What sets us apart?*

We Jesuits are men on a mission. We need carefully, prayerfully, and collaboratively to discern the needs we want to be missioned to meet, or, to put it another way, the direction in which our mission is to move. What set us apart historically was a conscious desire to serve where others were not serving, to meet needs, to help souls, to do what others could not do or chose not to do. It is up to us to decide now what will set us apart in future decades.

Being the best at what we do in meeting new opportunities or unmet needs (in the world that our assumptions say awaits us) is consistent with our founding vision. It is up to us now to "choose life" and to honor the trust the Society has placed in each of us and upon which the Society *lives*, to use the word that Peter Lippert chose to use.

Choosing life for us, it seems to me, will mean a number of things:

1. The Society will admit to the novitiate only those who are conscious of themselves as men called to celibacy.
2. Jesuits should work as a team, although teamwork will be more akin to performance on an American baseball team rather than other sports teams, because baseball requires individual execution of specific skills (e.g., batting and

pitching) in the company of, but separable from (and even substituting for) other members of the team. It is also a game where pitching twenty wins in a season or getting hits only one out of three times at bat is considered excellent performance. (There is a good lesson in that for Jesuits—those of us who worry about men leaving our ranks, those of us who inevitably strike out with some regularity, and those who won't do the practice needed to develop their apostolic skills.)

3. Jesuits should live in companionship but not at the price of removal from others whom the Society identifies as those to be served.
4. Jesuits should have mobility but recognize at the same time the value of an institutional base.
5. Given the rise of both the presence and the influence of lay men and women in the institutional life of the Church, Jesuits should be willing to relinquish managerial control of institutions and apostolates to lay leadership, preferring for themselves positions of influence in direct (e.g., teaching and counseling) and indirect (e.g., research and writing) service to others. Hence, there will be less urgency about preparing Jesuits for administration (allowing, however, for those who have the talent, and want to use it in administration, to do so), and more attention paid to preparing Jesuits for internal governance.
6. That Jesuit poverty should balance the need for witness to Gospel simplicity with the need for access to the tools necessary to do one's work, acknowledging that the need to give practical witness to Gospel values remains a challenge in an age of affluence for the privileged minority of the world's population in which we, for the most part, find ourselves.
7. That the catechesis of children (favored by St. Ignatius) might be revived in two forms in the United States: (1) Jesuits not otherwise committed pastorally on Sunday mornings might volunteer as instructors in parish religious education programs for children enrolled in non-Catholic schools, and (2) Jesuits could offer one-on-one religious

education for "children" who are no longer young—i.e. seniors living in retirement communities and nursing homes, whose religious literacy may be low. This might be an innovative way to recapture part of the Society's original commitment to catechesis.
8. Every Jesuit will feel obliged to respond as best he can to the challenge Father General Pedro Arrupe (1986, 74) gave us shortly before he died: "The first thing that all members of the Church, bishops as well as priests and lay people, expect from Jesuits is that they give the Exercises. This is the primordial task of the Society."

Choosing life will not be easy for Jesuits of the early twenty-first century, but it can be done and it certainly has a lot more appeal than the alternative.

I mentioned that Alfred North Whitehead once offered with approval this definition of a professor: "an ignorant man thinking." So I said to my British audience, "If you have found insufficient evidence of ignorance thus far in this presentation, just wait to hear my impressions of contemporary Church life in the UK." But that, of course, was why we were there—to discuss the future of Jesuit works in service to a changing Church in the United Kingdom. My ignorance needed the corrective balance of their observations and the direction that their assumptions could give to discussion of the future style and substance of the Jesuit "brand" as well as Jesuit works in England and Ireland.

My American Jesuit confrere Robert Drinan writes an opinion column regularly for the lay-edited U.S. weekly, the *National Catholic Reporter*. Knowing that I would soon be in England, I read with more than casual interest his piece in the September 24, 2004 issue. It appeared under the following headline: "The Melancholy Mood of English Catholics." Father Drinan's impression was gained from spending the month of July 2004 in London teaching a group of law students from Georgetown and several other universities.

His column paid customary respect to Cardinal Newman, Francis Thompson, Gerard Manley Hopkins, and Graham Greene before acknowledging his disappointment in witnessing "the gloom, even a certain malaise, in the English Church." Fr. Drinan went on to write: "The Jesuits seem to have a form of depression over the fact that the centuries-old Campion College [not to be confused with Campion Hall at Oxford] closed, *The Month* magazine ceased publication, and vocations are few. The jubilation of the 'second spring' in the restoration of the Catholic hierarchy memorialized by Cardinal Newman is a memory that seems to have no echoes at the moment." Most in my audience disagreed. Indeed, their Oxford meeting succeeded in stirring up or waking up those echoes.

There were, however, signs of hope noted by Fr. Drinan. These include liturgies at Farm Street, the "creative and resourceful" relationship between Heythrop and the University of London, and, although not a Jesuit enterprise, *The Tablet* is, in Fr. Drinan's view, a "universally respected" publication.

The negatives listed by this foreign observer represented opportunities for new ventures and future growth; if not growth in absolute numbers—of Jesuits and Jesuit works—at least new vitality in Jesuit activities. We all agreed that wishing won't make it so, but believing can have a lot to do with making it happen.

A more accurate and persuasive influence on my understanding of the contemporary Church in Britain came from David G. Barker's remarks at a lay-sponsored "Leadership Roundtable" meeting on "The Church in America" that I had attended at the Wharton School of Business at the University of Pennsylvania in June 2004. Mr. Barker was born in the United Kingdom, received his early education from the Marists, is an economics graduate of the University of London, and holds a doctorate in social administration. His career has been mainly in the management of charitable trusts.

THE CHURCH IN BRITAIN

David Barker's remarks at the Wharton School were based on a recent four-year study of the Catholic Church undertaken by the Queen's Foundation at Queen's College, Birmingham. The aim of this study was to assist the hierarchy in addressing the problems of "authority, governance, relationships, and participation in the

Church in Britain." Not surprisingly, as the findings make plain, the study focused on problems, not achievements. And the problems are the following:

The Laodicea Problem, a problem of complacency. In suggesting that the majority of British parents no longer value the transmission of religious faith to children, Barker quotes Jesuit moral theologian Fr. Jack Mahoney as saying, "the British are possessed of a vague religiosity which should not be probed too far."

The Legacy of Dependence. Until fifty years ago, says Barker, British Catholics were a "defensive religious minority" living in a closed social world "in which priests held power and the laity were," he quotes D. Ryan's (1986) book *The Catholic Parish*, "... pious, moral, docile, obedient—and passive. The ideal Catholic was the child." Still a minority (only one-tenth of the population), British Catholics, according to Barker, are assimilated into the majority population and share majority values. He notes that— not unrelated to this value shift—Mass attendance has fallen by half; priestly vocations have dropped by 60 percent in thirty-five years, and with the average age of bishops and priests rising, the clergy is finding it difficult to relate to young people.

Changed Attitudes to Authority. Barker says that individual conscience has displaced external authority as a source of moral judgment. People "seek authenticity, demand credentials, and want competence" from those in authority. British Catholics are also demanding accountability. And Mr. Barker quotes with approval Fr. Timothy Radcliff, former Master General of the Dominicans, who echoed Thomas Aquinas in saying, "The authority of the Church ultimately has to rely upon the truth of what we say—but truth born of lived experience." (I suggested that our closer collaboration with the laity extends our Jesuit reach into the desired lived experience. In other words, we have new eyes with which to see, new voices to attend to in our planning councils, and broader experiences than we could otherwise have had on our own.)

Changing Social Values. Dr. Barker finds a mismatch between dominant values in Britain today—"autonomy, equality, openness, empowerment, participation, tolerance, protest"—and the dominant values operative in the Church relative to laity, especially women, "as dependent upon the power and authority of an exclusively male priesthood."

Priesthood. Describing the Council of Trent's understanding of a priest as "a man set apart, celibate, and saintly," Dr. Barker uses Professor Eamonn Duffy's words to label that concept as "slowly collapsing under the joint pressures of theological and social change. [Hence there is] an urgent need to re-imagine the ordained priesthood as the Counter Reformation re-imagined and re-invented it." Meanwhile, the Church in Britain is experiencing what Barker describes as a sense of loss in the passing of the old order, and a weakened morale among its priests; "a middle-management gap caused by the defection of many able pastors," and a curious situation in which seminarians—who are being attracted by the dominant (but fading) ecclesiastical culture—are men who "do not relate easily to either their peers or parishioners." (By *peers,* he might mean seminarians who are ready to adapt to something new, or lay Catholics of the seminarians' own age. He probably means both.)

I learned from Dr. Barker that the Church in Britain numbers, in round figures, about five million Catholics in thirty-three hundred parishes; that there are about three thousand schools and colleges, including ten seminaries. There are thirty-eight bishops, seven thousand priests and deacons, about seven thousand nuns, and two hundred brothers, but he could offer no accurate estimate of the number of lay employees. I have no financial data.

According to Dr. Barker, British Catholics respect the person of the pope, bishop, and priest. The people "are typically loyal, concerned and supportive of the persons [of pope, bishop, and priest]," but they are "out of sympathy with the institution." They find much of Church teaching "impersonal, insensitive, out of touch, lacking compassion for those in difficult circumstances and sometimes in conflict with their consciences. They are dismayed by poor communication and scandalized by inaction and secrecy in cases of abuse."

There is a poor sense of mission in the Church in Britain, according to Barker. "British Catholics have a very poorly developed sense of the diocese as the local church and of its *Mission*," says Dr. Barker, "Indeed, the diocese is frequently seen as remote, inefficient and irrelevant to their lives." Why is this the case? Because the parish is the focus of church life and parishioners have little or no active engagement with their diocese. Moreover, "the authority of the bishop has been eroded both by social change and by centralisation in Rome.... Dioceses are geographically too large and sub-culturally too complex for the *communio model* to work effectively."

Disengaged, uninvolved, passive, unaware of diocesan priorities, spiritually unawakened, uninterested in faith development—this is Barker's broad-brush portrait of the British Catholic laity. And the discouraging picture is compounded by resistance to pastoral reorganization.

No small challenge for church leadership. No dearth of opportunities for a creative apostolic Jesuit response. But, if Barker is to be believed, the stimulus for change for more than a decade has been externally driven, not the work of Church leadership. "Changes in the Catholic Church in Britain which promote human well-being have not been pastoral or theological," he says, "They have been driven by the demands of the Civil Authorities. The dioceses have had to respond to government policy rather than offering courageous leadership."

The areas of change that he has in mind include "The Charity Law Reform Acts and Employment Legislation," calling for a complete review of diocesan accounting, financial stewardship, and administration; "Education Acts," resulting in significant changes in admissions procedures, curriculum design, financial management, and the measuring of attainment in Catholic schools; and "Social Policy Legislation," influencing diocesan child protection policies, provision for the disabled, and the functioning of diocesan welfare programs. What appears to be the case is that the state, not the church, is advancing an agenda that might have been prompted by Catholic social teaching, if that body of doctrine had been communicated. (Or, it is possible that the prompting for these changes came from public officials who had indeed been influenced by Catholic social thought. I just don't know.)

Given these changes, however, Dr. Barker finds a distortion in the allocation of human resources in diocesan curias. Professionals have been recruited in the change areas, but no corresponding developments have taken place to strengthen departments responsible for pastoral strategy. Finances are setting pastoral priorities. The Church, he says, "is not an exemplary employer," and is deficient, as an employer, in human relations skills.

ISSUES AND CHALLENGES

Finally, here is a list of issues and challenges with which Dr. Barker ends his assessment of the Church in Britain at the beginning of the twenty-first century:

- The Church has to learn to live with change while remaining optimistic and "having the courage to speak the truth ... and the charity not to collude with injustice."
- The institutional culture of the Church has to change from fear, secrecy, and control, to openness, dialogue, and co-responsibility.
- The Christian vocation needs redefinition and the priesthood needs reinvention.
- Attention must be paid to the theology and reality of the local church. "Bishops must take courage, acknowledge the current irrelevance of the diocese to Catholic life, and reclaim their legitimate status as the dynamic focus of the local church."
- Needed now above all are faith, hope, and optimism. "I wish to emphasise that, for many if not most Catholics, the difficulties they experience do not detract from their faith and commitment to Jesus Christ."

This leaves us with lots to think about, pray over, and discuss on our way to deciding *where* the Lord wants us (Jesuits and lay colleagues) to move and *what* the Lord wants us to do. The challenges in the United Kingdom are not all that different from the challenges in the United States.

Wherever we are in the world, we Jesuits know that our experience of the Spiritual Exercises contributes to whatever it is that sets us apart. We have a *substance* in faith and a *style* in our Jesuit way of proceeding. We know that the Society holds us responsible for the "service of faith and the promotion of justice." And we welcome lay collaboration in that mission. We also welcome our Jesuit call to assist lay Catholics in meeting their emerging mission of service in the Church. All of us have to help one another. All of us—Jesuits and lay colleagues—will have to deepen our bonds of friendship in the Lord while making the choices that will keep us faithful to our shared vocation.

I ended my Oxford presentation by sharing a reflection I had the foresight to bring along on the trip. I found signs of its continued relevance as I walked the streets of London for several days before moving on to Oxford for the conference.

Many years ago, when I was a summer editor at the Jesuit weekly *America* magazine, Father Thurston Davis, the editor, gave me a tear sheet from *The (London) Sunday Times Magazine* (May 27, 1962) and asked me to write a short editorial comment. I no longer have the comment, but I put the article in my files. The page-wide single-word headline reads, LONELINESS, and here are several paragraphs from that article:

> You don't notice them. Loneliness is a disease without physical symptoms. Only the victims know they suffer it: the bleak sensation of walking alone through a world of other people's friends. There is no clear sign of loneliness in the pretty girl idly window-gazing in the High Street, alone; the middle-aged shabby women lingering in teashops, alone; the dark, scattered figures in the Sunday afternoon cinemas, each alone; or the old men and women who blossom suddenly on park benches in the first spring sunshine, to sit waiting and watching for conversation, alone. You don't notice them, but there are more of them now than there have ever been.

> The number of lonely people in Britain has been rising steadily for the last twenty years. Today, general practitioners, psychiatrists, and social workers recognize it as an alarming iceberg of social malaise, in a country which is becoming steadily more impersonal as its mobility grows....

> In the dictionaries, solitude and loneliness are the same thing; in life they are not. Obviously, everyone needs some time to hear himself think. Some people are natural solitaries, content with their own company; or, if they believe they have one, with that of their God. Writers, painters, composers, require more solitude than most; heavy responsibility must to some extent set a man apart.
>
> But loneliness is not a chosen form of isolation. It is a sense of deprivation: the emptiness of the human being who longs for contact with others but who is, through circumstance or temperament, denied it. Solitude is an interval in living, but loneliness is a kind of death.

I suspected that much of this was still relevant in 2004, although the lonely may be less visible now, spending their idle hours in front of television sets, themselves out of view. They represent a pastoral opportunity for Jesuit ministry today. The liturgy, with good music and excellent preaching, can summon people out of their isolation and bring them together in community. This is, of course, a religious need but, upon examination, it can also be seen as a pressing social need that can be met through pastoral ministry. And the closer one gets to this problem, I said, the clearer it becomes that many of those most in need are not the elderly, but young men and women who will be open to creative initiatives that Jesuits and their lay associates might take in their direction.

It was more than interesting to me to hear, at the end of this two-day conference, an announcement by the provincial that the British Province would pay special attention to the eighteen- to thirty-six-year-old population as it focused its mission and shaped its ministries for the next half century.

5

■

A Church in Crisis

In any meeting, large or small, where American Catholics have gathered since 2002 to talk about the future, there is the eight-hundred-pound gorilla in the corner of the room. Sometimes it is in the direct center of the room. It is, of course, the clergy sex-abuse scandal.

The Wharton School meeting mentioned in the last chapter was one of many lay responses to that crisis. Several hundred Catholic business leaders formed a "Catholic Roundtable for Church Management" that meets annually for two days to discuss best practices—policies, and principles of management that must be adopted, in an atmosphere of transparency and accountability at all levels of organization in the Church, if past damage is to be repaired and future problems of mismanagement avoided.

Since 2002, I personally have been thinking systemically about a church in crisis. And I've been thinking in the context of structural adjustments on the way to new and better ways of managing parishes, dioceses, and other ecclesiastical organizations.

Sin, sickness, and crime are all part of the clergy sex-abuse revelations now tormenting the American Catholic mind. Shock, pain, anger, confusion, and outrage raise questions that have the Church searching for underlying causes. Blame is plentiful; analysis seems to be in shorter supply. The trust of the people is shaken. Demands are being made for transparency in ecclesiastical decision-making. The voice of the victim is, perhaps for the first time, clearly being heard. Unhealed wounds are exposed. The searchlight is now fixed on secrecy, arrogance, hypocrisy, incompetence, and the violation of trust. From church authorities, the wounded want apology, remorse, empathy, and justice.

From those not victimized directly, an interrogative chorus of *why, what if, why not, how could,* and *when will* is ringing out across the land. A wounded, but faithful, people of God wants to be a fully participating people in framing the questions and forming the answers. And the basic question is this: *What are we going to do now?*

I've listened to many of these people in open forums with parishioners, interviews with journalists, private conversations, and in letters and e-mail messages from both strangers and friends. I claim expertise on nothing beyond my own opinion and I presume to speak for no one but myself as I think about systemic, rather than surface, solutions.

What triggered this crisis was the public disclosure of reassignments, within the system, of a Boston priest—a known pedophile—to pastoral ministry. Multiple complaints. Multiple reassignments. Multiple instances of child molestation. The system provided medical, psychological, and pastoral care for the perpetrator, but apparently did not at that time recognize pedophilia as an incurable mental illness that fixates erotic attraction on prepubescent children. Nor, it seems, did the system acknowledge that pedophilia is in all cases a crime. Systemic breakdown on these two fronts is not likely to reoccur.

The illness is incurable. The sick priest must be barred from all unsupervised contact with children. The crime must be reported. That said, it is important not to label as a pedophile, a priest who molests minors, male or female, who are beyond the age of puberty. Such actions may be criminal and are certainly wrong and reprehensible. But the fate and future of this type of priest-offender can be different from that of the pedophile.

Every pedophile priest was once admitted, through the system, to a seminary, and after completing seminary studies, was admitted to holy orders. This raises the question of admissions standards—intellectual, physical, psychological, and spiritual fitness for the priesthood.

It is my opinion that a complete sexual history of the candidate must be known to the admitting authority at both thresholds—entrance to the seminary and admission to orders. This is delicate and difficult territory. Confessional matter may be involved. But disclosure would be voluntary on the part of the candidate, not released by a confessor in violation of the seal of confession.

The particularly sensitive matter of whether or not the candidate was himself abused sexually as a child or adolescent should be known. Not that this would be immediately disqualifying, but to insure that the psychological effects of that abuse have been dealt with successfully, and the probability of that person ever becoming an abuser is close to zero. Moreover, great care must be taken to reassure innocent victims of abuse that they are neither guilty nor responsible for what happened to them.

CREDENTIALING AND QUALITY ASSURANCE

What does the system tell the pastor and the parish community about the credentials and fitness of the priest it assigns to them for full- or part-time ministry? In most cases, not very much. Would it not be wise for every parish council to have a committee similar to the typical hospital's Credentialing and Quality Assurance Committee? Physicians have to present certified credentials before appointment to a medical staff. Their applications for appointment require disclosure of malpractice lawsuits, admonitions and the like, as well as their special competencies. Before it reaches the committee, an applicant's file is reviewed and approved by higher-ups like hospital section chiefs or department heads. There are obvious parallels to the review of clergy credentials before formal assignment to a parish. And the system could easily allow for periodic review of the credentials and performance of those already assigned.

Secrecy can be encouraged or discouraged in systemic fashion. The people are calling for transparency on the part of the Church in the way it deals will all issues related to this crisis. Transparency has not been a prominent part of the Catholic institutional culture with respect to the collection, distribution, and management of money. Now the culture is expected to open up and let the sun shine in with respect to sexual misconduct. Similarly, pressure is building for a more open and participatory selection process for bishops and pastors. This should not be mistaken for pressure to democratize. It is the expression of a deep desire to be informed and to be heard on the part of people in the pews who are intelligent and loyal, and who care deeply about their Church.

What a person does in secret is a disclosure of that person's character. In the development of priestly character, seminary guides should point out to their students what ethics professors point out to business students, namely, that a combination of three elements—secrecy, easy money, and the violation of trust—is all that is needed to trap the unsuspecting in a situation of business impropriety. Corruption in business or government begins with secret conversations focused on the tempting prospect of quick enrichment simply for looking the other way or cutting an ethical corner. And the price you pay, but try not to think about, is the violation of trust.

Sexual misconduct in the priesthood invariably involves secrecy, selfish pleasure, and an egregious violation of trust, not to mention the abuse of power and authority. It also involves the contradiction by the teacher of the Church's moral teaching, and the loss of moral integrity by a person ordained "to serve and not to be served." In business or in the Church, the system simply cannot sustain widespread violations of trust. It is no exaggeration to say that the Church is most alive in its parishes and that the parish lives on the trust it places in its parish priests.

Another systemic consideration in the present crisis touches upon the notion of ambition, an all too human quality that all too easily slips out of control. In my opinion, ambition is the poison at the bottom of the well in most cases of corruption in Church affairs. If promotion within the system is closed to those who speak up or write on controversial topics—regardless of how carefully, competently, and respectfully they articulate their views—those who rise to positions of leadership will be less likely to possess in full measure what Dennis Goulet once described as the three essential ingredients of Christian leadership: availability, accountability, and vulnerability.

Moreover, if ambition for higher and better positions possesses the heart of a priest, an otherwise good man will be inclined not to disclose regrettable past actions, which, although repented and forgiven, would be embarrassing and disqualifying if brought out into the light of day. In cases like these, one man's humble sacrifice of career ambition, will serve the Church in ways known only to himself and God.

Taking still another page from the business system, the Church might learn a helpful lesson from two contemporary business writers. One way to stop a business leader in his or her tracks, write consultants Robert Goffee and Gareth Jones (2000), is to ask: "Why Should Anyone Be Led by You?" That question is the title of an article these observers wrote for the *Harvard Business Review*. "Without fail," say the authors, "the response is a sudden, stunned hush. All you can hear are knees knocking."

The question is a good one to put to anyone in a leadership position anywhere. How would a cardinal, bishop, or pastor respond today? The reply has to be something more substantial than, "I've been assigned." Leadership implies voluntary followership. If you're the leader, why should I follow?

Goffee and Jones give a backward glance through history and acknowledge that there have been widely accepted leadership traits and styles. But they change over time. Today, they argue, the times require that "leaders should let their weaknesses be known. By exposing a measure of vulnerability, they make themselves approachable and show themselves to be human." Today's leaders, say these authors, have to adapt to "endless contingencies" while making decisions suited to a particular situation. They have to be "good situation sensors [able to] collect and interpret soft data."

Why should knees knock when a leader is asked, "Why should anyone be led by you?" If the so-called leader has specialized in unavailability, unaccountability, and presumed invulnerability, the question could be quite discomfiting. Those in leadership positions in the Church today should be wise enough to ask themselves why they are there. And those who constitute the followership can exercise their own quiet leadership by raising that question ever so gently whenever circumstances warrant it.

All should clearly understand that authority and leadership are not the same thing. The authority conferred by sacrament and system on a priest or bishop is not now being questioned; it is whether or not the person in authority possesses the ability to lead.

The names we call ourselves provide perspective on how we conduct ourselves within any system. I've been called *father* now since 1961 in the system of ordained priestly service to the Catholic community. When a child, speaking of me, asked her mother, "Whose father is he?" the mother, a young widow whom I had helped when her husband, a former student of mine, was killed in an automobile accident, found herself saying, "Anybody who needs one."

A male pastor can be father to his people without being paternalistic. Some lay Catholics and not a few non-Catholics are uncomfortable with the term. I'd trade it for *pastor* in the united Church we all pray for, where Lutheran pastors and female ministers would not have to stumble over awkward nomenclature. Regrettably, we are not even close to having to deal with that question now. All monsignors are still safe!

A perhaps apocryphal story told about a now deceased "prince of the Church" has the reverend gentleman, a cardinal, speaking to his assembled priests and communicating to them a point that emerged from his morning prayer. "I asked our blessed Lord this morning what I should do about this," said the cardinal, "and Our Lord said to me, 'Your Eminence...'"

Why did everyone, except the prelate, laugh?

SERVANT LEADERS

There is something of a flattening out, a de-layering, taking place in the Church today. It is not an erosion of authority. It is an emergence of humanity, human leadership, what some are calling *servant leadership*. It is a movement of the Spirit bringing leadership and followership closer together in the community called the Church.

"I am Joseph, your brother," said the late Joseph Cardinal Bernardin when he met for the first time his assembled priests in their cathedral in Chicago. Not Joe, but Joseph. Many priests, and some laypersons too, addressed him that way during his years of service to the Church in Chicago.

Visitors to the cemetery at St. John's, the Benedictine Monastery in Collegeville, Minnesota, walk up a path and see, on the hill above, stump-like granite crosses over the graves of the monks. Carved onto the back of the crossbar is the first name only. It meets the eye as the visitor approaches. *Michael, Godfrey, Robert*. Strong, stark, dignified, solemn. I would not be surprised to see a gradual shift over the years from an emphasis on formal ecclesiastical titles to simple and straightforward baptismal names in correspondence and conversation between the faithful and those ordained to serve them from positions of authority in the Church.

There is a deeply felt need among lay men and women in the church to be seen and heard by those in authority. There is a poignancy in their plea for improved communication. Some few are strident and demanding, but more, if I am not misinterpreting the voices I'm hearing, are loyal and loving in their insistence on being heard. It is something like the "mounting urgency" that the stage directions expect of Emily in Thornton Wilder's "Our Town" when, toward the end of the play, she says, "O Mama, just look at me one minute as though you really saw me.... Mama, just for a moment.... *Let's look at one another.*"

Celibacy invariably comes up as people try to puzzle their way through news reports dealing with the present crisis. So does the question of ordination of women. The system permits neither women—nor married—priests at the moment, as we all know, and there is systematic suppression of open discussion of these issues. Change, if it comes at all, is a long way off. The crisis we have to confront is of the present moment, however, and both time and emotional energy spent on debating (or demanding) change in these rules is energy and time not spent on addressing the question of what might be done now.

Both issues—optional celibacy for priests, and the ordination of women—cannot, however, be simply dismissed. Nor, in my opinion, is it dispositive to say that the ordination of women is impossible in the Catholic faith community. If, as Mathew tells us, Jesus said, "For God, all things are possible" (Matt. 19:26), there may indeed one day be alternatives to an all-celibate, all-male Catholic priesthood. This is not a case of squaring a circle. But we know where Pope John Paul II stood on these questions; we don't know where his successors will line up. We can be sure, however, that much prayer, discussion, and exploration of the historical, theological, anthropological, psychological, and sociological dimensions of these issues is needed. Addressing these questions calls for scholarship now. They should not be systematically excluded from consideration. Debate and diplomacy may, if the Holy Spirit moves these questions forward, come later.

Meanwhile, we should be very clear about a few more things. There is no credible evidence that pedophilia is disproportionately a Catholic clergy problem compared with males in other professions and clergy in other denominations. There is no causal link between celibacy and pedophilia and no evidence that celibacy, for those capable of making that commitment, contributes to other forms of clergy sexual misconduct.

Nor is there any causal connection between pedophilia and homosexuality. There may indeed be more men of homosexual orientation in the ranks of Catholic clergy now than was the case a generation or more ago. But sexual orientation is not the issue; keeping one's commitment to celibacy is. Celibacy is not the cause of the present crisis. Recommitment to celibacy can be part of the solution.

Even if optional celibacy for diocesan or "secular" priests becomes a feature of Catholic life, celibacy will still be an organizing principle (not the only one, of course, but an important one) for community life in religious orders like the Benedictines, Dominicans, Franciscans, and Jesuits. And as we all know, St. Peter had a mother-in-law. Celibacy for diocesan priests came later, as a disciplinary requirement with a functional purpose related to priestly availability and service. If it is seen by the Church as no longer necessary for its intended purpose (a not unimportant *if*) the discipline is likely to change.

CHANGE WITHIN THE SYSTEM

How, *within* the system, will any change come about? On a major issue like ordination of women, the forum for discussion and debate would most likely be an ecumenical council, a worldwide gathering of bishops and their advisers, both clerical and lay. Any pope may call an ecumenical council for consultation on any number of questions affecting the life of the Church. Optional celibacy for priests and ordination of women may or may not be on the agenda of the next council. A praying, discerning Church, ready to respond to whatever God wills, will, under the guidance of the Spirit, decide those questions in due time. It must not, however, permit itself ever to stifle systemically the voice of the Holy Spirit on matters of deep concern to the people of God.

Catholics have to recognize that in the present crisis, we are all in this together. Some are guilty; all are responsible. I mean all Catholics, laity and clergy, are responsible in the sense that a collective response is required. And the magnitude of this crisis is such that it requires, in my view, a response of prayer and fasting to call down the healing power of God.

Money is another matter very much on the minds of concerned Catholics in this present crisis. Some are calling upon others in the faith community to withhold financial contributions to dioceses where scandal has hit but transparency has yet to arrive. I think a better and more honest protest would be to associate one's name with the contribution, but designate the protester's gift to help the poor, or to be passed through by the diocese to a nearby Carmelite or Trappist monastery where the prayer and fasting that this crisis calls for are part of the vocation lived out there every day.

Money—in large amounts—is also mentioned in reports of settlements with victims, leading to speculation about possible bankruptcy and to the unanswerable question of how much money can ever make a victim "whole." Since enormous amounts of money are involved, prudence requires church officials to seek the advice of lawyers. Victims turn to lawyers. The Church needs lawyers too for protection against false claims and assistance in pursuing a just resolution of complaints. But lawyers must never have the only or the final word. We must remain open to the voice and direction of God.

St. Paul wrote to the Romans, "Where sin abounds, grace abounds all the more" (Rom. 5:20). Sinful actions and sinful structures have overwhelmed us in recent years. Grace will abound, indeed abounds right now, and will carry us through this crisis into a promised future.

6

■

Protecting Children from Pornography on the Internet

During the summer of 2000, Richard L. Thornburgh, former governor of Pennsylvania and later the U.S. attorney general, recruited me to serve on a committee he was assembling in response to a Congressional request to initiate a study that would develop "tools and strategies" to protect children from pornography on the Internet. Thornburgh, then out of government and working as a private-sector lawyer based in Washington, DC, was invited to chair this effort with the help of staff from the National Research Council, the operating arm of the private, not-for-profit National Academies. The Academies provide independent advice to the government and the general public on public policy matters related to science, technology, and medicine.

"Youth, Pornography, and the Internet," (2002), is the product of the committee's work. Committee members included academics and practitioners, librarians, and computer scientists. Among them are the head of the national Parent Teachers Association; a former law dean who is an expert on the First Amendment; the chief operating officer of the National Center for Missing & Exploited Children; a research psychologist; the former editor in chief of *FamilyPC Magazine*;

and two consultants who follow business development in cyberspace (one of them protects bank clients from computer hackers). I was there because of experience teaching business ethics and social responsibilities of business in the college classroom. (I jokingly accused Governor Thornburgh, whom I had known for many years, of selecting me in order to make sure someone older than he was was on the panel, and so that he and I together could lower the Internet IQ of the group to a "we the people" level!)

The committee conducted hearings, commissioned study papers, and made site visits to middle schools, high schools, and libraries around the country. Its final report caught the attention of the wire services, National Public Radio, *USA Today*, and several trade magazines, but it did not get the attention I thought it would receive in the major daily newspapers.

At our organizational meeting in Washington, each member of the committee was asked, in keeping with National Academies policy, to disclose any biases and real or potential conflicts of interest (e.g., the likelihood of benefiting financially from findings the committee might publish). I recall saying that I had two biases and no potential conflicts. I was pessimistic, I said, about the possibility of significantly reducing this problem, given the permissiveness of our First Amendment culture. I also expressed a personal preference for creativity over censorship, but admitted that displacing sex and violence with positive values like love and courage in the new world of Internet imagery would be an uphill struggle.

A QUESTION OF CHARACTER

Now these many years later, I'm convinced that there is no technical solution and that the challenge is reducible to a question of character. Just as children have to learn what is good or bad for them in the consumption of food and drink, they have to be encouraged to internalize the values that will prompt them to consume no inappropriate Internet imagery, reject hate speech and other offensive messages delivered on computer screens, and, most important of all, be aware of the perils of participation in chat rooms.

The committee's report sends this message to the American public:

> To date, most of the efforts to protect children from inappropriate sexually explicit material on the Internet have focused on technology-based tools such as filters and legal prohibitions or regulation.... While both technology and public policy have important roles to play, social and educational strategies to develop in minors an ethic of responsible choice, and the skills to effectuate these choices and to cope with exposure, are foundational to protecting children from negative effects....
>
> Though some might wish otherwise, no single approach—technical, legal, economic, or educational—will be sufficient. Rather, an effective framework for protecting our children from inappropriate materials and experiences on the Internet will require a balanced composite of all of these elements, and real progress will require forward movement on all of these fronts.

These words are neither a white flag raised nor a towel tossed in. Balance and forward movement are possible. Common sense will drive progress. Enforcement of existing laws will help. New laws are on the way. But at the end of this very long day, personal character is our last best hope. Sadly, the report has relatively little that is new to offer by way of social and educational strategies, and that deficit surely signals a need for more research and development along those lines at many levels across the nation.

It is important to note that the concern that launched this project is not the criminal problem of child pornography. This committee dealt with protecting children from exposure, via the Internet, to products of the "adult entertainment" industry, to all inappropriate sexually explicit material, and to potentially dangerous experiences occasioned by use of the Internet.

The delivery channels for these dangers are Web pages, e-mail, chat rooms, instant messages (IM), Usenet, and peer-to-peer connections. Strategies targeting only Web sites will fall far short of the goal.

IM is private one-on-one text-based dialogue; it can contain links to objectionable material. Usenet is a worldwide network of newsgroups (also called forums or message boards) covering, at the time our committee was at work, an estimated forty thousand different topics. Users can post anything they care to, and often do so anonymously. The committee reported that "the sexually explicit content on Usenet newsgroups is often more extreme than those on adult-oriented Web sites." Moreover, sexually explicit Usenet newsgroups are conduits for advertising adult-oriented Web sites and can provide their users with a mechanism to swap sexually explicit material. Some Internet service providers (ISPs) carry a full line of Usenet newsgroups.

A peer-to-peer connection is made without the mediation of a central server. They are generally not anonymous and typically are employed for file sharing, including free files with sexually explicit content—no proof of age necessary.

The lengthy report of the committee covers a broad range of topics including technology; the economics of adult online entertainment; legal and regulatory issues; the impact of sexually explicit material on children; and tools for dealing with the problem that draw on technology (filters and blocks), the law, law enforcement, and social and educational prevention strategies that relate to the formation of character.

The committee's work generated more reflection and discussion than controversy and condemnation. Not surprisingly, not everyone agreed with every word in the report. Constructive criticism came from readers who wanted more regulation. Complaints came from those who faulted the report for tolerating too much control. But out of the conversation that this report stimulated, ideas emerged that can be implemented in homes, public and private schools and libraries, and in government agencies and private businesses. And the spotlight (searchlight?) focused on the enormous challenge in all this for legitimate business—especially the Internet service providers, dot-com entrepreneurs, and the credit-card industry—to be socially responsible.

PARENTAL INVOLVEMENT

I have no way of knowing how many parents responded to the report's call for more parental involvement—supervising (not snooping), encouraging youngsters to alert their parents and talk to them about objectionable images, and insisting that the computer be kept in an open space (a hallway or family room), not in a youngster's bedroom.

The report is good at staking out the reasons why any parent of any healthy, normal child should be concerned:

> The years between pre-adolescence and late adolescence are often turbulent times, in which youth struggle to develop their own identities. They are eager to be heard, seen, and taken seriously, but often lack the experience and maturity to make responsible choices consistently. They test boundaries in developing their emerging adult personalities, and they take risks that adults would deem unwise. They are often socially uncertain, and they value peer approval highly. And in pre- and early adolescence, hormonal changes generally stimulate their interest in sexual matters. Because of the intensely personal nature of such matters (both sexual and social), the "at a distance" nature of Internet communication and the anonymity with which one can seek out a great variety of information on the Internet is highly appealing to very social but also sensitive individuals.

Everyone is aware that youngsters know more about the Internet than their parents and spend far more time online than their elders do. Less well-known, however, is the fact that young people go online more for health information than for shopping, chatting, or downloading music. There are technological tools to help a parent find where a youngster is going online, but privacy considerations and principles of positive parenting suggest that the most effective way to find out is simply to ask. As one observer noted, "Keeping a child out of harm's way on the Internet has as much to do with a parent's ability to talk openly with a child as it does with how computer savvy a parent is."

On the First Amendment issue, it is helpful to be clear that this Constitutional guarantee of freedom of expression protects a citizen only from government, and does not apply to private homes or private cultural or educational institutions. Kids have no First Amendment rights against their parents! Public schools and public libraries are, however, "government" in First Amendment matters. Yet, the committee report, acknowledging that the Supreme Court allows for a two-tier applicability of First Amendment protection to children, notes, "the government can prohibit children from having access to certain types of sexually explicit material that it cannot constitutionally ban for adults." This relates to a doctrine of "variable obscenity" that enables government constitutionally to ban minors "from buying, renting or viewing certain sexually explicit movies and magazines that would not be obscene for adults." This is much easier to apply when you can individuate the audience—at the box office or in the bookstore, for example. It is more difficult to apply to television, radio, and the Internet. Filter designers have to face up to this problem.

Public librarians can be libertarian (as one told the committee, "a tap on the shoulder" [of an adult viewing a pornographic Web site in open library space where passing children could see the screen] would be "Constitutionally questionable." Or, public librarians can be diplomatic in monitoring for possible abuse, and creative in providing attractive, filtered content for kids in the children's section of the library.

What a person does in secret tells you a lot about that person's character. The committee favors openness over secrecy and looks to character development as a key protective strategy. "The role of ethical and moral education is to articulate guiding principles for the child that can be freely chosen and, once internalized, serve to prompt appropriate behavior." The right values "can serve to help a child judge what is or is not reasonable in a context broader than the immediacy of pleasure and pain, of 'getting caught' or 'getting away with it.'"

For years, Stephen R. Covey's (1989) *The Seven Habits of Highly Effective People* has dominated the best-seller lists. Largely forgotten is that book's subtitle, *Restoring the Character Ethic*. Now it seems that restoration of the character ethic is the recommended route to be taken by anyone interested in waging a defensive strategy in the battle against pornography.

# 7

Organizational Ethics

Restoration of the character ethic was on my mind when I responded to an invitation from the Catholic Health Association to give a keynote speech titled "Beyond Corporate Compliance: Touching the Source of Our Integrity," at the Catholic Health Assembly in Chicago, on June 7, 2004. The theme of the meeting was organizational ethics. The program planners asked the membership of healthcare administrators and business managers to think beyond corporate compliance as they examined together the source of their integrity. The focus of this assembly was not on medical ethics or bioethics, but on business ethics in healthcare organizations.

I began by saying that I think of integrity in terms of wholeness, solidity of character, honesty, trustworthiness, and responsibility. And when I think of organizational ethics, two notions come immediately to mind. One is culture; the other is trust. Before commenting on those two notions, however, I thought it might interest my audience first to learn about a conversation I had about organizational ethics a few months earlier with James E. Burke, former chairman of the board of Johnson & Johnson, who is admired worldwide as a model of integrity for his 1982 decision to pull Tylenol from drug store shelves everywhere because a few Tylenol capsules were found to be laced with cyanide that caused seven deaths in the Chicago area.

When I asked Mr. Burke to tell me how he understands integrity, he summarized it all in one word—trust. He said,

Tylenol was driven by a belief I had. There was no question as to what I had to do, and what the company had to do. There were people in the company who questioned me, and there were those who disagreed with me. But there was no question in my mind. You can't put a product on the market that killed seven people and not take responsibility for it. And the best way to take responsibility for it is to get rid of it and give the public what they should have had in the first place. The Tylenol case is a classic example of where trust worked.

People felt that the company could be trusted when I took that product off the market. I think it was a $56 million business then. That was an enormous sacrifice to make. I think the business now is $1.8 billion. It couldn't have happened, of course, without the fact that the public trusted us and trusted Tylenol. My whole claim in these areas is that trust is not only the only way, but it also works.

And Jim Burke added, "The reason I stick with the trust thing is that it simplifies it all."

CULTURE AND TRUST

With that as preamble, I turned to the notions of culture and trust. The late Canadian Jesuit theologian Bernard Lonergan defined or described culture as "a set of shared meanings and values." "There are as many different cultures," according to Lonergan, "as there are different sets of shared meanings and values."

So, I suggested that this audience of about fifteen hundred healthcare administrators think first of organizational culture before getting to the specifics of organizational ethics. What is the culture that characterizes the organization? You should be able to find a clue to this in the organization's mission statement. Cultures are defined by dominant values, so it is important to identify the dominant value that defines the culture of the organization before examining the ethics of the organization. And, of course, that dominant value should find expression in the organization's mission statement. (In his conversation with me, James Burke made repeated references to the famous Johnson & Johnson Credo.)

For a simple, down-to-earth, practical illustration of articulating a dominant value, I would refer anyone to a summer camp for boys in Westport, in upstate New York, on the shore of Lake Champlain. Camp Dudley has been there since 1885. Founded by the YMCA, it is now an independent corporation governed by a board of trustees, and operates as a non-denominational Christian camp for boys, ages seven to fifteen, under a motto that expresses the dominant value and thus defines the culture of this camp. That motto is: "The Other Fellow First."

I spend a long weekend at Dudley every summer as a guest chaplain—one of a number of guest clergy, male and female, of different Christian denominations—to lead a noon Sunday interfaith chapel service in an outdoor "chapel" of long-log "benches" on a tree-lined slope running down to a bluff that overlooks the lake. There is a platform there equipped with lectern, microphone, organ, and chairs for readers, cantors, and the leader of prayer who is also the chapel speaker.

Some years ago my visit to Dudley coincided with Parents' Weekend. Soon after arriving on Friday afternoon, I happened to meet a couple from New York City who had come to visit their eight-year-old son. He was experiencing his first extended stay away from home. His parents mentioned that their boy had encountered a few adjustment problems in his Upper East Side private elementary school and they were anxious to see how he was getting along at camp. A few minutes later the youngster, a bit overweight, came waddling up to greet his parents. He was introduced to me and just to make a bit of ice-breaking conversation I asked, "What do you like best about Camp Dudley?" His immediate response: "Nobody here makes fun of you."

That response says a lot about culture shaping behavior. It also suggests the wisdom of encapsulating the organization's central value in a motto that conveys the organization's culture. Jesuit schools say they are educating "men and women for others." The U.S. Army invites you to "be all that you can be." Hewlett-Packard does things "the H-P way." "Cornellcares.com" is one medical center's Web address offering innovative tools, strategies, and advice related to geriatric mental health. The Web address expresses a value wrapped in a slogan: "Cornell cares."

And so it goes throughout the world of slogan communication here on earth and out in Cyberspace.

Much more could be said about culture and capturing values in mottos, but I chose to move on at that point to the notion of trust.

The journal of the Public Relations Society of America is called *The Public Relations Strategist*. The cover of its Fall 2003 issue calls attention to "Corporate America's New Secret Weapon: Trust." The cover story, written by Joanne DeLavan Reichardt (2003), vice president of corporate communications and public affairs for Ranstad North America, opens as follows: "Trust has seldom been more top of mind in America's break rooms, board rooms and corner offices than it is now. In fact, we are in the midst of a crisis of confidence when it comes to trust, one that has profound implications for us as social human beings and as professional communicators." The article goes on to say that mistrust is pervasive. "We've seen it in politics, with special favors exchanged for political contributions. We've seen it in sports, with investigations of cheating or lying by university coaches and Little League teams that falsify birth certificates of star players. We've certainly seen it in business, with accounting fraud scandals."

The author omitted any reference to scandals in the Catholic Church or church-related institutions. But this audience of professionals serving in church-related institutions or in any form of church administration knew that the Church has an enormous organizational ethics problem on its hands and that we have to learn, as this article puts it, that "the building blocks of trust are consistency, clarity, courage, and a willingness to handle difficult issues."

There were in the business press in 2002, headlines, news stories, and editorials that might just as easily have found a place in the Catholic press.

"Stop Stonewalling on Reform," reads the scolding June 17, 2002 editorial. "Each day brings news of yet another...scandal." "A Ripe Time for Reform," was the headline over an editorial in an earlier issue of the same magazine. It opened with the words, "The ground is shifting beneath the foundations of..." and I left it to the audience to complete that sentence. They could easily err in completing it, because this is *Business Week*, not *America*, *Commonweal*, or the *National Catholic Reporter* that I'm citing. American business, not the Catholic Church in America, is the object of this editorial criticism of stonewalling and the absence of reform.

Consider the front cover of *Business Week* (May 6, 2002): "The Crisis in Corporate Governance: Excessive Pay; Weak Leadership; Corrupt Analysts; Complacent Boards; Questionable Accounting; How to Fix the System."

One week later the same magazine had this on its cover: "Wall Street: How Corrupt Is It?" On Feb. 25, 2002, *Business Week's* cover story pointed to "betrayed" investors who have been "misled by Wall Street, corporations, accountants and the government. The strength of the recovery hinges on winning back their confidence."

Finally, the June 24, 2002 *Business Week* cover highlighted a "Special Report" on "Restoring Trust in Corporate America: Why CEOs Must Speak Up; How Institutional Investors Are Pushing Reform."

The Church can learn a lot from what analysts say about corporate corruption. Religious commentators call the clergy sex-abuse scandal the most serious crisis the Catholic Church in America ever faced. *Business Week's* May 6 report says, "Faith in corporate America hasn't been so strained since the early 1900s when the public's furor over the monopoly powers of big business led to years of trust busting by Theodore Roosevelt." The parallels are striking. Substitute *bishop* for *CEO*, and *diocese* for *corporation* as you read these accounts of the predicament in which the American business system finds itself. There is "widespread suspicion and distrust" in both arenas where decision-makers have committed "egregious breaches of trust"—words taken from the business press, but applicable on the ecclesiastical side of the street.

No small embarrassment for the Church to find itself compared with Enron and Arthur Andersen. Ironically, the Andersen CEO used religious language to explain his resignation as a *sacrifice* for the good of his employees.

Writer Thomas Keneally says that he separated himself from the ranks of practicing Catholics years ago when he became convinced that "behind the compelling mystery of Catholicism...lay a cold and largely self-interested corporate institution." The executives of that *corporate institution*, the bishops—not yet ready to perform surgery on themselves in Dallas at their June 2002 meeting—returned home to their chanceries faced with the challenge of trying to repair the damage and prevent further harm.

Some are pushing reform. Most, having heard the victims tell their stories, are closer to their people and realize that recovery hinges on winning back their confidence.

Although the bishops know that their corporate institution has a soul and lives on God's promise to be with the Church until the end of time, they are now—especially since the release of the National Review Board's root-cause-analysis paper on February 27, 2004—thinking systemically. They can learn from what the business system has done and is doing in its effort to recapture lost trust. Transparency, accountability, reform of governance, servant leadership, and patient listening are coming to the rescue of the business system. All of these, along with humility, penance, and prayer provide a formula to be followed by all who love the Church enough to change it. Our Church will become stronger in its broken places if executive courage, not executive privilege, becomes the order of everyday ecclesiastical life. And this, it goes without saying, applies to everyday organizational life in church-related organizations. And it is in this context that I spoke to this Chicago audience about organizational ethics in a church-related institution.

For more than two years, I told them, I had been at work on a project I think of as a study of "old ethical principles for the new corporate culture." It was in connection with that study that I spoke to James Burke a few months earlier. I listed these old ethical principles and invited the assembled healthcare administrators to consider how the principles apply in the organizational culture from which they came to this meeting and to which they would return within a day or two.

THE PRINCIPLES

I encouraged them to come up with their own understanding of each of the principles I was about to name. It was important, I said, for them to articulate their own understandings of these matters and to assess how widely shared, in their home organization, are the understandings each has of these classic principles. To repeat what I noted earlier by quoting Lonergan: a culture is a set of shared meanings and values. How widely shared, I asked, are your meanings and values relative to the following ten points?

The Principle of Integrity. As I said when I mentioned earlier my conversation with James Burke, I think of integrity in terms of wholeness, solidity of character, honesty, trustworthiness, responsibility. What would you add or subtract from that understanding?

The Principle of Veracity. Veracity to me involves telling the truth and it also includes accountability and transparency.

The Principle of Fairness. By fairness, of course, I mean justice, treating equals equally, giving to everyone his or her due.

The Principle of Human Dignity. Acknowledging a person's inherent worth is the bedrock principle of all ethics—personal and organizational. It prompts respectful recognition of another's value simply for being human.

The Principle of Participation. In this case, the principle of workplace participation respects another's right not to be ignored on the job or shut out from decision-making within the organization.

The Principle of Commitment. What I have in mind is that a committed person can be counted on for dependability, reliability, fidelity, loyalty.

The Principle of Social Responsibility. Social responsibility points to an obligation to look to the interests of the broader community and to treat the community as a stakeholder in what the organization does.

The Principle of the Common Good. A sense of the common good operates as an antidote to individualism; it aligns one's personal interests with the community's well-being. This may indeed be the most difficult of all these principles around which to form an organizational consensus relating to the common good of the organization and then relating that understanding to an understanding of the broader common good outside the organization.

The Principle of Subsidiarity. Subsidiarity can be understood in terms of delegation and decentralization, keeping decision-making close to the ground. It means that no decision should be taken at a higher level that can be made as effectively and efficiently at a lower level in the organization. This could be viewed as a "principle of respect for proper autonomy." It could also be understood in terms of Saul Alinsky's "Iron Rule" for his Industrial Areas Foundation: "Never, never do for others what they can do for themselves."

The Principle of Love. Love, as a principle, is an internalized conviction that prompts a willingness to sacrifice one's time, convenience, and a share of one's material goods for the benefit of others.

I later (2006) developed all ten of these into a book, *The Power of Principles: Ethics in the New Corporate Culture*. The Chicago meeting and several subsequent presentations to health-system administrators helped considerably in shaping my ideas for that book.

It is a commonplace to note that the search for organizational ethics will lead directly to the corner office, to the executive suite, to the person and character of the CEO. And that raises a question that I raised but did not explore, namely, the presence or absence of a direct connection between the personal morality in the private life of the CEO, on the one hand, and, on the other, the organizational morality in the public moral person of a corporation, institution, or organized collection of the many persons, who, working under the leadership of a CEO, try to achieve an organizational purpose.

I prescind from the question of whether a man who is unfaithful to his wife can lead an ethical organization, or whether a woman who habitually lies to a friend can lead her organization to a high and consistent level of ethical integrity. It is easy to judge, but hard to measure the correlation between the personal character of the leader and the institutional integrity of the organization. It is a question worthy of careful consideration and study, however.

Writing in the *Wall Street Journal* on January 23, 2004, Jack Welch, the retired chairman of GE, spoke of the "four essential traits of leadership." He listed them as (1) energy; (2) the ability to energize others; (3) having an edge ("the courage to make tough yes-or-no decisions—no maybes"); and (4) the ability to execute. If a candidate for a leadership role has all four of these, says Welch, "then you look for a final trait—passion. By that I mean a heartfelt, deep and authentic excitement about life and work." But, according to Welch, you cannot even start to think about the Four E's until you get a solid yes on two questions:

> First: Does the leadership candidate have integrity? That means, does he or she tell the truth, take responsibility for past actions, admit mistakes and fix them? Does he demonstrate fairness, loyalty, goodness, compassion? Does she listen to others? Does he truly value human dignity and voice? These may seem like fuzzy, subjective questions, but you have to get a strong Amen in your gut to all of them to even consider a person as a leader.
>
> Second: Before applying the Four E's, you have to ask, is the candidate intelligent? That doesn't mean a leader must have read Kant and Shakespeare.... It does mean the candidate has to have the breadth of knowledge, from history to science, which allows him to lead other smart people in a world that is getting more complex by the minute. Further, a leader's intelligence has to have a strong emotional component. He has to have high levels of self-awareness, maturity and self-control. She must be able to withstand the heat, handle setbacks and, when those lucky moments arise, enjoy success with equal parts of joy and humility.

When the Catholic Health Association invited me to give this presentation, the Martha Stewart trial was underway. In her opening remarks to the jury, Assistant U. S. Attorney Karen Patton Seymour said: "Ladies and gentlemen, lying to federal agents, obstructing justice, committing perjury, fabricating evidence, and cheating investors in the stock market—these are serious crimes." Indeed they are. And although her organization—Martha Stewart Living Omnimedia, Inc.—was not on trial, the faults and failures of Martha Stewart raised questions about the ethics of the organization she headed.

Around that same time, Paul Krugman's February 8, 2004 *New York Times* review of two books "about CEOs who looted their companies and the financial press that covered up for them," opened with these words:

> Eighteen months ago, American capitalism seemed to be in crisis. Stocks had plunged, and some of the nation's most celebrated business leaders had been exposed as phonies if not crooks. Now the economy is growing, and the Dow's been back above 10,000.... So is it safe to buy stocks again? After you read Roger Lowenstein's [2004] *Origins of the Crash* and Maggie Mahar's [2004] *Bull!*, you'll have serious doubts. Both tell the story, from different angles, of how ordinary investors got suckered into supporting the lifestyle of the rich and shameless. And you have to wonder whether anything has really changed.

Krugman's review goes on to say: "Lowenstein's title may convey the impression that his book is mainly about stock prices. It isn't: it's about the epidemic of corruption that spread through corporate America in the 1990s, though that epidemic was in part both an effect and a cause of the bull market. A better title might have been *Executives Gone Wild*."

Do these leaders have integrity? Hardly. Do their organizations embody high levels of organizational ethics? Not likely. Part of the problem, in the case of errant CEOs, is a lack of oversight on the part of governing boards, and where wrongdoing occurred at lower ranks of executive responsibility, the problem is a failure of higher-ups to monitor what was going on below them.

THROUGH AN ETHICAL LENS

With the help of accrediting organizations, auditors, and outside directors, healthcare administrators can look at themselves and their organizations through an ethical lens. (In my view, accreditation is not as helpful on that score as it should be.)

The trustees of colleges and universities also have to face the issue of organizational ethics, and that process begins with a thorough examination of their own conduct. *The Chronicle of Higher Education* carried a page-one story on February 6, 2004 under a headline that read: "Boards Crack Down on Members' Insider Deals," with this accompanying subhead: "Recent scandals trigger new scrutiny of trustees." The story mentioned that Auburn University, the University of Idaho, Boston University, and the University of Georgia Foundation were under investigation for questionable business ties between trustees and the institutions they serve. "In an earlier era," says *The Chronicle*, "the awarding of sweetheart business deals by boards to their members and members' companies, a practice widely known as self-dealing, was often accepted with a wink and a nod. To avoid the appearance of impropriety, trustees usually just recused themselves from votes on matters in which they would benefit, a provision that did not always curb conflicts of interest."

Sometimes in the spirit of *noblesse oblige*, often for purely altruistic motives, and occasionally in an unholy community-service competition with their peers, business executives have been known to covet a board-membership trifecta that connects them to a bank, a hospital, and a university. To the extent that mixed or self-serving motives bring such a member to a seat on a healthcare governing board, an administrator has to be wary of ethics erosion becoming a problem in his or her organization.

It all comes back to culture and trust. What is the dominant value that defines the workplace culture? How widely is it shared throughout the organization? How trustworthy are leaders in an organization? How trustworthy are they perceived to be by those they lead in that organization? How fully encompassing is the trust that generates the energy and purifies the air of the organization that has a claim on the administrator's time, talent, and commitment?

Trust is something of an elusive concept that is perhaps more easily understood in a healthcare setting than in other areas of corporate activity that depend, as do healthcare organizations, on trust for their long-term viability. Think, for example, of the trust a bedridden patient places in physicians, nurses, and other healthcare providers with whom they come in immediate contact. What is the substance, the texture, the fabric of a trusting patient-provider relationship?

Competence—being very good at what you do—is part of that relationship from the side of the provider, as is the provider's integrity, veracity, dependability, and availability. From the side of the patient, cooperation and honesty are two important strands in the relationship. Both competence and cooperation are integral to the relationship of trust, and that relationship is strengthened by integrity, veracity, dependability, availability, and honesty.

How can this reality, this kind of trust, become part of the life of your organization? It begins with persons and it has to begin with the small things—the courtesies, the reliabilities, the acknowledgments, and a genuine institutional humility. In the person of the CEO—the occupant of the corner office—there must be what Dennis Goulet has called "availability, accountability, and vulnerability." If you've been there, you will understand what he means by vulnerability. If you have been an effective CEO, you will agree that availability and accountability belong in your executive toolkit.

Two additional healthcare analogies might be helpful. One is preventive medicine. You cannot afford to wait until trust is lost to begin thinking about the maintenance and preservation of trust in your organization. Preventive measures in preserving both personal health and organizational trust are always less costly and more effective than waiting for a crisis to arise and then deciding to deal with it.

TRUST BANK

The other analogy looks to health insurance. It is captured in the term *trust bank* coined forty years ago by Al Golin (2003). He is author of *Trust or Consequences: Build Trust Today or Lose Your Market Tomorrow*. "Just as you wouldn't go without health insurance because you're physically fit, you shouldn't go without a trust bank just because your organization has good values," says Golin. And what is a trust bank? "As the name implies, a trust bank involves making deposits of good deeds into an account over time that can be drawn upon in times of need." This suggests that the organization should be doing good deeds for its employees, its clients or customers, and in its surrounding community. Organizational generosity can build organizational trust.

Think for a moment of all associates in a given organization. Think of them within the framework of trust. Recognize that the organization cannot operate without social trust, without the social collaboration of human beings. "The way you create trust," says Kenneth Dunn (2004, 91), dean of the business school at Carnegie Mellon, "is to have complete transparency of your decisions."

Is yours a high-trust, low-trust, or no-trust organization? Listen to Francis Fukuyama (1995, 6–7), whose book, *Trust: The Social Virtues and the Creation of Prosperity*, reminds us:

> While people work in organizations to satisfy their individual needs, the workplace always draws people out of their private lives and connects them to a wider social world. That connectedness is not just a means to the end of earning a paycheck but an important end of human life itself. For just as people are selfish, a side of the human personality craves being part of larger communities. Human beings feel an acute sense of unease...in the absence of norms and rules binding them to others, an unease that the modern workplace serves to moderate and overcome.
>
> The satisfaction we derive from being connected to others in the workplace grows out of a fundamental human desire for recognition. ...Every human being seeks to have his or her dignity recognized...by other human beings. Indeed this drive is so deep and fundamental that it is one of the chief motors of the entire human historical process.... This kind of recognition cannot be achieved by individuals; it can come about only in a social context.

> Thus, economic activity represents a crucial part of social life. ...One of the most important lessons we can learn from an examination of economic life is that a nation's well-being [I would substitute, *a healthcare organization's well-being*], as well as its ability to compete, is conditioned by a single, pervasive cultural characteristic: the level of trust inherent in the society [or, as I would suggest, *the level of trust inherent in the healthcare organization*].

If a healthcare organization is a caring community built on a foundation of mutual trust, it will be conducting its affairs far beyond the low-altitude horizons of corporate compliance, and it will have found the source of its corporate integrity.

I ended my Chicago talk with a parting reflection prompted by our Catholic liturgical return at that time in early June to Ordinary Time and our remembrance on the day before I spoke, of those who lost their lives in France on D-day exactly sixty years earlier, as well as the death two days earlier of President Ronald Reagan. I noted that we just concluded the liturgical celebration of the events that combine to form what we call the Paschal Mystery—the death, resurrection, and ascension of Jesus. The Paschal Mystery is the pattern for our lives. We know that we move through death to life, through defeat to victory, through sadness to joy. The Risen Lord is always with us. It is not that we have picked a winner, but that a winner—an eternal winner—has picked us, I said.

The Church in America over the previous two years experienced in the disclosures of the clergy sex-abuse scandals the *death* side, the downside of the Paschal Mystery. The upside—the *resurrection* and *new life* side—is coming, I said. I acknowledged that I don't know exactly when, but it is coming. And I'm convinced that in the vanguard, in the front ranks of that upside revival in the Church, will be women—women like those who have built Catholic healthcare and Catholic education in the United States. Religious women and laywomen will be there at the leadership level. I'm convinced of that.

We are a people of hope, I said, as I thanked everyone in that assembly for the hope they bring to this moment in the life of the Church. There is a lot that we can look forward to on the upside of our experience—as a Church in healthcare and other ministries—in the new life that will be ours with the Spirit who is leading us into our unknown future. And I added this: All we can do is follow. All that we can be is faithful and grateful.

8

■

Courage and Competence

I've long thought of courage and competence as overlooked virtues in the search for corporate integrity. And I took this impression with me to the University of Portland in June, 2005, when I participated in a conference there on "Teaching, Faith, and Service." In a presentation made at that meeting, I had the opportunity to think out loud along lines traced out earlier for me by former Pennsylvania governor and U.S. Attorney General Richard L. Thornburgh (who prefers, even in formal print, to be called Dick), whom I mentioned earlier in this book.

Dick Thornburgh served as court-appointed examiner in the WorldCom Bankruptcy Proceedings. In December 2003, he gave his reflections on that experience in a speech at a dinner meeting of the Committee on Federal Regulation of Securities of the American Bar Association. Thornburgh saw WorldCom as "a kind of poster child for corporate governance failures in this new century." There was, he said, "the failure of directors to recognize, and deal effectively with, abuses [that reflected] a 'culture of greed' within the corporation's top management. ...The company overstated its income by approximately $11 billion, overstated its balance sheet by approximately $75 billion and, as a result, caused losses in shareholder value of as much as $250 billion." Thornburgh went on to say this:

> Our investigation concludes that WorldCom was dominated by Bernard Ebbers and Scott Sullivan, the former chief executive officer and chief financial officer of the company, respectively, with virtually no checks

or restraints placed on their actions by the board of directors or other management. Significantly, although many present or former officers and directors of WorldCom told us that they had misgivings at the time regarding decisions or actions by Mr. Ebbers or Mr. Sullivan during the relevant period, there is no evidence that any of these officers and directors made any attempts to curb, stop, or challenge the conduct they deemed questionable and inappropriate. Instead...it appears that the company's officers and directors went along with Mr. Ebbers and Mr. Sullivan, even under circumstances that suggested corporate actions were at best imprudent, and at worst inappropriate and fraudulent....

In fact, several multi-billion dollar acquisitions were approved by the board of directors following discussions that lasted for thirty minutes or less and without the directors receiving a single piece of paper on the terms or implications of the transactions....

Our investigation raised significant concerns regarding the circumstances surrounding the company's loan of more than $400 million to Mr. Ebbers. As detailed in our reports, the compensation and stock option committee of the board of directors agreed to provide enormous loans and a separate guaranty for Mr. Ebbers without initially informing the full board or taking appropriate steps to protect the company. Further, as the loans and guaranty increased, the committee failed to perform appropriate due diligence that would have demonstrated that the collateral offered by Mr. Ebbers was grossly inadequate to support the company's extension of credit to him, in light of his substantial other loans and obligations. Our investigation reflected that the board was similarly at fault for not raising any questions about the loans and merely adopting, without meaningful consideration, the recommendations of the compensation committee.

MINIMUM PARTICIPATION REQUIREMENTS

Not raising any questions? Without meaningful consideration? Those are minimum participation requirements for any board of directors. Mr. Thornburgh concluded:

> Next only in importance to the absence of internal controls as a cause of this debacle was the lack of transparency between senior management and the board of directors at WorldCom....I believe that this failing helped to foster an environment and culture that permitted the fraud to grow dramatically. A culture and internal processes that discourage or implicitly forbid scrutiny and detailed questioning are breeding grounds for fraudulent misdeeds. In tandem with the accounting irregularities, these shortcomings fostered the illusion that WorldCom was far more healthy and successful than it actually was during the relevant period.

Ultimately, they also produced massive investor losses, bankruptcy for WorldCom, and a profound loss of confidence in our financial markets and economic system.

WorldCom's directors were, according to the court-appointed examiner, "all too often a passive rubber stamp for management and especially Mr. Ebbers."

Is it an exaggeration to say that all of this could have been avoided if the board had done its job? Perhaps. But it is no exaggeration to say—as Mr. Thornburgh did when he participated in a panel discussion on corporate governance in late 2004 at Georgetown University's Woodstock Theological Center—that "a culture that emphasizes ethical conduct will make more difference than all the laws and regulations promulgated by various government agencies." He acknowledged that the temptation is always there to view additional statutory and regulatory enactments as government-imposed impediments to smooth and efficient corporate governance, but he does not agree. "I think Sarbanes-Oxley and similar initiatives will empower the 'good guys,' and there are plenty of them out there in the business system, far more than the few bad apples that spoiled WorldCom and Enron."

Although Dick Thornburgh mentioned (almost in passing) in his 2003 American Bar Association speech that liability for corporate directors "is still a developing field," and that "recent court decisions have already pointed to an expanded potential for directors' liability," neither he nor anyone else was ready to predict what actually happened on March 18, 2005. That was the day of final approval of a landmark agreement by eleven former independent directors of WorldCom to pay $20 million out of their own pockets to settle a civil suit representing hundreds of thousands of investors whose WorldCom holdings became worthless when the company went bankrupt in 2002. The investors succeeded in holding the directors accountable for mismanagement and fraud that happened under their watch. The settlement with the directors came in the same week that WorldCom's founder and CEO, Bernard J. Ebbers, was found guilty of directing the $11 billion accounting fraud that took the company down.

Think of Enron's Ken Lay or WorldCom's Bernie Ebbers against the background of Robert Greenleaf's (1977) observation in his famous book *Servant Leadership*: "To be a lone chief atop a pyramid is abnormal and corrupting.... When someone is moved atop a pyramid, that person no longer has colleagues, only subordinates. Even the frankest and bravest of subordinates do not talk with their boss in that same way that they talk with colleagues who are equals, and normal communication patterns become warped." A strong, participating—i.e., fully informed, fully awake, outspoken and questioning—governing board is needed to correct that abnormality and prevent possible corruption. Greenleaf thinks that the title, *chief executive officer*, "and the single-chief concept it conveys, should disappear as an anachronism." It will come as no surprise that Greenleaf believes that "no one, absolutely no one, is to be entrusted with the operational use of power without the close oversight of fully functioning trustees."

I offer all of this by way of preamble—admittedly, a fairly lengthy preamble—to my reflections on courage and competence as often overlooked values or virtues in our continuing quest for integrity in the corporate world. A question about both, but especially courage, has to be raised when one asks what in the world the WorldCom board was doing while Bernie Ebbers was destroying that company.

I was on that panel with Governor Thornburgh at Georgetown; we were joined by Tom Saporito, an international business consultant who specializes in board selection and corporate governance. After each of us had spoken, and before questions came from the audience, each of us was asked by the moderator to make a one-minute summary statement. We were meeting in the library of the Woodstock Theological Center; off to the side, but within clear view of the audience, was a bust of John Courtney Murray, the great Woodstock theologian who was the principal architect of the Second Vatican Council's famous document on religious freedom. As I looked at the sculpted head of Father Murray mounted nearby, I recalled that his Jesuit colleague of many years at Woodstock, Fr. Walter Burghardt, told me more than once that Murray used to say to him during difficult or stressful times, "Courage, Walter, it's far more important than intelligence!" I repeated that in my summary comment and underscored the importance of courage on the part of corporate directors if debacles like Enron and WorldCom are to be avoided in the future.

When once asked which characteristic he most admired in other people, Karl Rahner, another great Jesuit theologian, said simply: "Decency, courage, cheerfulness, helpfulness, fidelity." When are all those qualities going to find their way into the job descriptions and personality profiles of corporate executives?

GOVERNANCE IS GOVERNANCE

During my presentation on that Woodstock panel, I had mentioned Bill George's (2003) book *Authentic Leadership*. I recommend it to anyone interested in getting caught up on the preventive role good governance can play in avoiding corporate scandals. The author is former chairman and CEO of Medtronic. His title selection for his fifteenth chapter says it all: "Governance Is Governance." Don't talk about it; do it. Participate in governance and the job will get done. George takes the reader inside the boardroom and describes how "good governance lies in the chemistry between the board and the CEO." Wait a minute, I hear you saying, isn't that the problem—cozy chemistry? It could be, but the right chemistry means awareness on the CEO's part that the board is in charge. It also means that there is both comfort and courage at the board level to raise any question, to request any report, and not to be intimidated by the powerful personalities of top managers.

Although a clique of outside directors can bond too closely with a strong-willed CEO (if they happen to constitute the executive compensation committee, as is often the case, the chemistry will surely be counterproductive), strong independent directors have to be ready to speak up, speak out, risk unpopularity in the board room, and, as one from the oil services industry once said to me, "you always have to be ready to shoot that snake as soon as you spot it moving through the grass."

Outside, or independent, directors should meet alone from time to time. One of them should, if the CEO is also board chair, head up an independent governance committee and be designated as the board's *presiding director* with power to call and chair executive sessions held in the absence of management and other inside directors.

I think devices like these are necessary because I agree with a view expressed to me by veteran CPA John Coughlan:

> Management, through the proxy process (so often underutilized and passive), owns the board of directors, and through the board, it owns the outside accountant. Members of the board are well compensated. They know their continued presence on the board and their prospects for serving on other boards depend on their willingness to go along. I read somewhere that Vernon Jordan, in addition to being a partner in a prestigious law firm, serves on eleven boards of directors. Meaningful service on a board requires at least two hundred hours per year, so eleven boards would raise that requirement to at least twenty-two hundred hours, leaving little time for an important law practice.

Coughlan wrapped up this reflection by saying, "In management's view, the 'good' directors are those that turn up for meetings, read the *Wall Street Journal*, and only pay attention when the chairperson calls for a vote. And if the chairperson pulls his or her right ear, they vote Yea, and if it's the left ear, Nay."

Participation in a strong, ethical, well-functioning business corporation moves from top to bottom, bottom to top, and all across the organization. Governance guides the operation; management executes. Under the broad canopy of the principle of participation, those up there at the very top are the board members. The search for tone at the top has to reach higher than top management; it has to look to the board of directors. Some notable failures to participate at this level are part of the sad story of corporate wrongdoing and collapse in the earliest years of the present century.

Governance is, by definition, participation. Not to participate is not to meet the responsibilities of governance. And I'm convinced that ethical analysis of governance failures will often reveal an absence of courage. Speaking of board responsibility, a lawyer friend remarked to me, "You never want to be in a position where you would have to admit that the question occurred to you, but you just didn't ask it." He was talking, of course, about the absence of courage.

To engage itself honestly and effectively with the issue of organizational ethics, a board of directors has to first take a good look at itself, as is happening in corporate America in the wake of Sarbanes-Oxley. Some boards are under investigation for questionable business ties between directors and the corporations they serve. The awarding of sweetheart business deals by boards to their members and members' companies, a practice that goes by the name of self-dealing, still goes on with token avoidance of the appearance of impropriety by permitting directors to recuse themselves from votes on matters in which they would benefit financially. To the extent that mixed or self-serving motives bring a director to a seat on a governing board, it is likely that an erosion of ethics will become a problem for the organization.

After describing, in *Origins of the Crash*, the problems that triggered several of the major corporate scandals in recent years, Roger Lowenstein (2004) writes: "It is fair to wonder why directors went along with such abuses, and the answer has its roots in the distinct culture of America's boardrooms." Elements of that culture are the twinning of the positions of chairman and CEO in one person ("Think how inappropriate would the description President and Chief Justice sound, or Head Coach and Quarterback," Lowenstein says.); the fraternal character of boardrooms (Lowenstein calls them "modern oases of gentility"); long tenure; interlocking directorships (so that the watchers were also being watched by those they were overseeing); use of compensation consultants whose recommended salary hikes for the CEO would boost the average against which outside directors, who were also CEOs, would have their compensation compared; and an accepted boardroom etiquette where, in Warren Buffet's words, to stand up and criticize the CEO felt like "belching at the table."

COMPETENCE IS AN ETHICAL CONSIDERATION

In addition to courage, I would also propose *competence* as an ethical consideration that has received insufficient attention in the nation's hand-wringing search for solutions to corporate corruption. There is an ethical obligation to be competent—very good at what you do—if you hold a position of executive responsibility. Not only do the careers and retirement security of a lot of people on a given CEO's payroll depend on it, the safety and satisfaction of those who meet the CEO's product or service in the marketplace presume competence to be there on the other side of the exchange. Incompetence is a form of lying. In one-on-one encounters, it is usually evident. But in large organizations, not knowing the right thing to do or not being able to tell the truth because the matter is too complicated to understand, are deficits to be overcome before the simple act of telling the truth can come to the rescue. There are a lot of incompetent people behind the corporate scandals of recent years—brilliant in some respects, but incompetent in important areas of leadership responsibility. Not to narrow the range of incompetence unduly, it can surely be said that The Hall of Shame would include CEOs who knew nothing about ethics and directors who knew nothing about accounting. Relative to both of those fields of knowledge, ethics and accounting, they were simply incompetent.

Competence, of course, means mastery; it follows upon days, weeks, usually years of study and practice. Competence is not a gift; it is an achievement. Competence comes only to those who are willing to work for it. Directors who consider board membership an honor, and executives whose position at or near the top is viewed as an entitlement, hold titles that are almost always unsupported by the competence required to do the job.

The notion of competence figured prominently in a dialogue on corporate leadership at the University of Notre Dame, April 14–16, 1980. Elmer W. Johnson, then a senior partner of Kirkland & Ellis, a 250-member law firm with offices in Chicago and Washington, DC, was one of the speakers. He mentioned that he had been assigned by his firm to write up a set of criteria by which partners in the firm might be measured over the long term for compensation purposes. He viewed the criteria as describing his "ideal of a top partner of a large law firm, which, with a few modifications, describe my ideal of a top executive of a large corporation." At the top of the list is professional competence. He described it in these words: "The partner will be measured first and foremost on the basis of technical competence in the partner's particular field of expertise, peripheral vision in perceiving legal problems outside the partner's field of expertise that call for attention of others in the firm, readiness to seek from and provide others in the firm such professional consultation as will serve the clients' best interests, and creativity and imagination in solving client problems."

I should add that the other criteria were personality and cooperation, judgment, productivity, leadership, and external representation. Johnson presumed moral character to be associated with each criterion. And in spelling out in a bit more detail his understanding of competence, Elmer Johnson said, "First, the pursuit of competence calls for self-discipline. It has been my experience that the top lawyer or corporate executive or leader in any other organization who has a high degree of competence is a person who is slightly monastic. The self-indulgent hedonist is unlikely to develop great competence."

I've made reference several times in this chapter to the importance of participation in the workplace. I think of workplace participation as an ethical principle, one that merits inclusion in this discussion. Once accepted as an operating principle within the organization—i.e., as a prominent feature of the organization's culture—a commitment to participation will prompt management to include employees in the process of decision-making that could affect them adversely. A good example would be the decision to outsource certain functions. Colleges and universities, for example, are increasingly turning to outsourcing as a way to improve efficiency and enhance revenue in activities like the bookstore, food services, printing, and other areas. "Outsourcing Can Make Sense, but Proceed with Caution" is the headline advice over an article on this topic in the *Chronicle of Higher Education*. Author Paul Davis (2005), drawing on his past experience as director of finance and auxiliary services at Duke University, advises: "Be straightforward with employees about outsourcing, and try to speak before the rumor mill speaks for you."

Cutting rumors off at the pass makes for both lower blood pressure and higher productivity in the workplace. Speaking in advance of both rumors and actual decisions is good management practice. Since participation in this context applies to those who are likely to be affected adversely by an outsourcing decision—e.g., bookstore clerks as well as managers, cafeteria workers, and veteran printers now on the university payroll—it is important that they have precise information on the options that might be taken, and a voice in deciding which option is best for the organization overall. Then they'll be informed participants in the next stage of decision-making, namely, whether there is a continuation-of-employment opportunity for them with the new contractor, and, if not, whether some training to update and enhance skills (as well as outplacement services) will be available to them during the transition.

Participation is a form of recognition that is appreciated by persons at all levels of an organization. As other forms of recognition dry up because of potential conflicts of interest and ethics-code bans on receipt of gifts or entertainment beyond token value, managers have to be more attentive to legitimate forms of recognition. And this can be a challenge. Let me simply say that if competence is present, participation will be there. And the presence of participation may open up new challenges for executive courage!

PriceWaterhouseCoopers took out a full-page advertisement in major newspapers in January 2005 to say that every corporation needs a *chief courage officer*. Not a bad idea. It is not likely to happen, however, even though many corporations are appointing chief ethics officers and their portfolio will be carried more gracefully and effectively if the person bearing the title is a person of courage. I think courage has to be part of the corporate culture; it has to be a shared value. If courage is a dominant value helping to shape a corporate culture, an act of courage on the part of one individual will draw both a positive reaction and imitation from others in the organization. And it should go without saying that, without competence, the organization simply cannot deliver on its promises and will not be what it claims to be. That's an ethical challenge that will take a lot of courage, on the part of those confronted with it, to overcome.

9

Reasoned Argument about Abortion

I once heard Hillary Clinton say, "I think abortion is wrong, but I also think women should be free to choose." She may have said "morally wrong"; I don't recall precisely. Undoubtedly, Mrs. Clinton was thinking within the "safe, legal, and rare" framework her husband had sketched out for the abortion issue during his first presidential campaign.

We were in a small, informal conversation group—about ten or twelve—as the first term of the Bill Clinton presidency neared its midpoint. "We don't want to have happen to us what happened to the Carters," said Mrs. Clinton. And by that, of course, she meant a one-term presidency, going down to defeat two years later in their bid for re-election. So she inquired about building better relations with various ethnic and interest groups, including Catholics, and it was in that context that the abortion question came up.

I asked whether they had had any recent contact with then Pennsylvania Governor Robert P. Casey, who, presumably because of his outspoken defense of unborn human life, was denied an opportunity to speak two years earlier at the national convention that nominated Mr. Clinton. "Well, we make sure to let him know when we're coming into Pennsylvania," she replied. It crossed my mind that any Pennsylvanian reading the daily press would know when the President was going to visit the Keystone State. So I mentioned the possibility of a more direct and personal outreach to the politically popular, Catholic, pro-life Democratic governor, who happened to be a personal friend of mine.

This prompted the First Lady to ask how the abortion debate might be raised to a more civil, constructive, and respectful level of discourse. And that got me thinking about the usefulness of inserting the adjective *moral* between *pro* and *choice*. Let's all be pro—i.e., *for* or *in support of*—any moral choice.

I suggested that Mrs. Clinton might invite the pro-life side of the debate to elaborate moral arguments (as opposed to arguments from authority, or arguments based on emotion, fear, or threat) for their position. And I added that she should think about articulating a moral argument for her position on choice. All of us should be able to say we are *pro* any possible moral choice. The challenge, of course, lies in making the moral argument. Not to attempt to make that argument would be irresponsible, in my view, given the seriousness of the issue.

Now, many years later, in the aftermath of a presidential election in 2004 that appears to have turned to some significant extent on moral values, Senator Hillary Rodham Clinton found herself at the leadership level of a Democratic Party in disarray. Governor Casey said repeatedly before his death in 2000 that the party was "losing its soul" by refusing to make room in its policy deliberations, its national platform, or on its presidential ticket, for a moderate pro-life position. It seemed to me in 2004 that the party might want to begin an internal recovery process by engaging so-called pro-choice and pro-life Democrats in conversations within the Democratic family on questions of narrowing the legal range of permissibility of abortion to cases of rape, incest, or the life of the mother; and removing any criminal penalty from a ban on abortion. That has not yet happened.

Narrowing the range of permissibility would bring the matter closer to what I believe is the national consensus on protection of unborn human life. But just raising this question triggers opposition from defenders of a woman's unrestricted "right to choose" to terminate the life within her womb at any stage of the pregnancy.

Some conscientious persons may not equate human personhood with human life at its earliest stage of existence, but there is no denying that "it" is alive and will, if permitted to continue living, become a fully human person. As Bob Casey used to say, "It certainly isn't going to become a rhinoceros!"

NO CRIMINAL PENALTIES

Removing criminal penalties would, in my view, show a respect for both freedom of choice (moral choice, remember) and freedom of conscience on the part of those who see life, but not human life, and the potential for personhood, but not an actual person, in a human embryo. I can disagree with those who see neither human life nor the potential for human personhood in an embryo, but still respect the dignity of those who, in good conscience, hold that view.

Does life-protecting law without a criminal penalty make sense? I think it can. Let politicians and lawmakers debate over criminalizing or decriminalizing so-called partial-birth abortion and you will find that room is being made for pro-choice candidates to support a ban on partial-birth abortion, which they see as morally indefensible, while still permitting first trimester abortions, which they may personally oppose on moral grounds but permit on political grounds out of respect for those who, apparently in good conscience, disagree. To be clear, let me say that I oppose abortion under any circumstances, but am willing to yield some ground here to those who conscientiously disagree, in the hope that the compromise—not on principle but on policy—would mean a significant reduction in abortions in America.

Conversations and debates along these lines within the party will bring opposing positions up to the higher and common ground of respect for human life. This would, I believe, strengthen the party's united convictions about improving things for the poor; avoiding unnecessary war; eliminating capital punishment; saving Social Security; advancing medical research; containing medical costs while extending medical coverage; improving the quality, efficiency, and effectiveness of education; defending the right of workers to organize and bargain collectively;

assisting immigrants; protecting the human and civil rights of all minorities; and assuring justice in law enforcement, taxation, and employment.

NEW VOCABULARY NEEDED

Observers say the moral value question of same-sex marriage figured in the outcome of the presidential election in 2004. In dealing with this issue, neither party can afford to substitute political correctness for political courage. Respect for and courageous defense of human dignity is central to this debate. Redefining marriage is not a solution. What is needed is a new term that defines a committed, permanent, same-sex union in a way that gives each partner an enforceable claim to the rights and benefits that marriage confers on spouses relative to hospital emergency room and intensive care visits, inheritance, insurance, and similar matters. Would *sharriage* catch the meaning of a permanent commitment to share one's life with another of the same sex? Might that partner be described as a *sharand*? Is there a better term waiting to be discovered that could describe this relationship reality without invading or preempting the meaning of *marriage*? Would those most immediately affected by denial of these rights now be open to the introduction of a new term? Would those who condemn homosexual acts as immoral, be similarly open? Who knows? Perhaps the word *marriage* sounded awkward and strange to those who heard it when it first dropped into our vocabulary! Those who believe, as I do, that a homosexual orientation is morally neutral, homosexual acts are morally wrong, and homosexuals are fully human persons whose dignity and rights deserve protection and respect, need a workable vocabulary to enter into the conversation.

It certainly won't be easy, but no progress will be made if the discussion takes place in a vacant vocabulary outside the range of reasoned argument. Nor will it help if each side simply aims pre-recorded messages at the other. It is time now to listen and talk to one another with respect. And this takes me back to the abortion question.

In a speech at the University of Notre Dame in 1995, Bob Casey said abortion is "like a bone in our throat. We can't swallow it. We cannot assimilate it. We cannot become comfortable with it, because it's fundamentally contrary to what we believe as Americans.... Every poll shows a vast and growing unease with the abortion license and the industry that serves it. I believe a pro-life consensus already exists in America. And it grows every time someone looks at a sonogram." Reason, not religion, brought him to this conclusion. Reasoned argument will lead to conclusions that can be commended to all because of their consistency with the human nature shared by all, not necessarily because of their conformity with the tenets of a religion to which not all subscribe.

Whether the pro-life consensus Casey saw still is or ever was there, Democrats are going to have to look for an answer to this question within their own tradition of concern for the poor and vulnerable. If a consensus is there, they can find it and build on it. If not, they might think about developing one for the good of the nation, not just the good of the party. As the Jesuit theologian John Courtney Murray used to say, echoing the Dominican philosopher Thomas Gilby, civilizations rest on citizens locked in argument.

Democrats don't apologize for big government so long as it is a positive influence that does for citizens what they cannot effectively or efficiently do for themselves. The unborn cannot do anything for themselves. It would be a beautiful irony if debate over meeting the needs of the unborn could now become the route the party takes back to the winner's circle in national elections.

To brush this consideration aside as idealistic and impractical would be to miss the truth that there is, on occasion, nothing so practical as the right ideal. This moment in the nation's political history may be such an occasion.

An ideal capable of bringing more unity (and in unity is strength!) to Democrats is the principle of respect for human dignity. Applied evenly across the board, this principle can not only revive a party, but position it to make its own unique contribution to building a better nation through the give and take of politics.

10

Seeking Justice, Ending Hunger

As one who was present at the creation, so to speak, of Bread for the World (BFW), I was asked by Carlos Navarro, the leader of BFW in New Mexico, to visit Albuquerque in 2004 for a celebration of Bread for the World's thirtieth birthday. He asked me to speak about the origins and founding vision of this Christian citizens' movement, the voice for the voiceless poor and hungry, that is known as Bread for the World.

In the early seventies, I met Arthur Simon, who was then an associate pastor at Trinity Lutheran Church in a poor neighborhood on the Lower East Side of New York City. I was teaching social ethics at Woodstock, the Jesuit seminary, and at the Protestant Union Theological Seminary on the Upper West Side of Manhattan. Art Simon and I were both part of what was known as the Inter-Religious Coalition of New York Clergy, a loosely organized advocacy group made up mostly of Protestant social-action types left over from the civil rights movement of the fifties and sixties. We met for a brown-bag lunch about once a month, discussed issues of importance to the faith-justice community, and, on occasion, took some direct action. When, for example, a white policeman shot a black teenager on a street in Queens and there was a threat of violence breaking out the next night, three members of the Clergy Coalition—a Protestant minister, a Jewish rabbi, and I, a Catholic priest—visited the Queens District Attorney to work out a reconciliation with the minority community.

At one of the Clergy Coalition luncheons, Art Simon invited me to meet with him and several others once monthly, over the next few months, to help him develop and clarify a general idea he had for helping the poor. He and his brother Paul, who later became a U.S. senator from Illinois, had published a book on poverty and public policy. Art was wondering if it would be possible to borrow John Gardner's Common Cause model, apply it to the Christian interfaith community, and address in some way the problem of poverty.

I clearly recall a meeting one night in Art's fifth-floor, walkup "railroad flat" on Avenue B near Twelfth Street in lower Manhattan. I remember, when the door closed behind me, seeing a wooden pole connected to the back of the door that fit into a brass inset hole in the floor and thus served to reinforce the door against someone who might want to push it down and break into the apartment. Not a safe neighborhood!

HUNGER IS THE MOST URGENT FORM OF POVERTY

That evening in that apartment we came to a helpful, clarifying insight—nothing extraordinary, just helpfully clarifying—that hunger is the most urgent form of poverty. Instead of focusing on poverty, we thought, it might be best to focus on hunger. Moreover, as we gave it more thought, it became obvious that hunger was a good ecumenical issue, capable of bringing together believers from left, right, and center on the Christian spectrum. You couldn't do that if the issue were nuclear disarmament, unemployment, welfare reform, or war and peace. But people of faith with partisan and ideological differences will respond to hunger and work together to eliminate it.

Our strategy was to begin with small groups of believers—we decided early on to limit this movement to Christians so that we could hold their feet to the fire of Gospel passages relating to concern for the poor and hungry—small groups of believers who could come together for shared prayer and reflection on what the Bible, particularly the New Testament has to say about care for the hungry.

We knew that, sooner rather than later, those who gathered in non-Eucharistic communities to pray in this way, would begin to reflect on the causes of hunger, and start asking what might be done about the problem, and indeed what might they themselves be doing about it. So we thought of advocacy on behalf of the hungry poor, advocacy that would be geographically rooted in Congressional districts. Our dream was to have at least one BFW chapter in every Congressional district in the country. We laid down parallel tracks, if you will—one reaching into faith communities; the other running through every one of our 435 Congressional districts.

People in the prayer groups did begin to ask what they might do. Chapters began to be formed. Membership grew. And now we have members in 55,000 households and congregations all across the country.

Let's go back for a moment to the foundational insight: Hunger is the most urgent form of poverty. Hunger in the human family is a scandal, a disgrace, a problem that can be solved.

We believe that all of creation is a table set by God to meet the needs of men and women everywhere at all times. Everyone has a faith-reinforced human right to be there. "For the promise that he would inherit the world did not come to Abraham or to his descendants through the law but through the righteousness of faith" (Rom. 4:13). We, the faithful, are called to do what we can to make sure that all our brothers and sisters in the human community (broadly speaking, the descendants of Abraham) receive their share of the inheritance, have their place at the table, enjoy their portion of the meal.

That is the mission of Bread for the World, which, as I indicated, is a faith-based lobby for the hungry poor. Advocacy is the BFW style. BFW members who, by their membership, participate in that mission are demonstrating their fidelity to the call to discipleship.

Members of the Holy Trinity Catholic Parish Community in the Georgetown section of Washington, DC, when I served as their pastor from 2000 to 2003, passed under an overhead sign as they left church on Sundays that reminded them of the challenge of Matthew 25 by asking: "Lord, when did we see you hungry?"

On Monday mornings they went back to work on Capitol Hill, in the White House, in law firms, trade associations, and lobbying organizations where they found themselves wondering how, from those observation posts, they could *see* and *do something* for the hungry poor.

Those who grow discouraged in the face of mounting world hunger and poverty can find consolation in the Genesis 18 story of Abraham and Sarah welcoming the three men sent to them by the Lord. In particular, the fourteenth verse of that chapter is one that should be permitted to sink into the soul, roll around the mind like a mantra, be internalized as a guiding principle, and become a deeply held conviction: "Is anything too wonderful for the Lord?"

Cannot the Lord work any wonder? Is anything impossible for God? Yes, the Lord can work wonders. No, nothing is impossible for God. Why then, does hunger still persist? Because, we have to admit, God chooses to work with human hands. And humanity's hands, including our own, have not applied themselves effectively to the task of eliminating hunger and balancing the worldwide scales of justice. We tolerate injustice. We permit poverty.

I think of poverty as sustained deprivation. The poor are deprived of many things, food being one of them. Our inactivity helps to sustain their deprivation.

We don't know anything about the three men who visited Sarah and Abraham. Their mysterious presence in this story lets us speculate on the way God communicates with us, to ask who it might be today who carries God's messages to us, to wonder about the ways in which we might read God's will in the faces, words, and events surrounding us in the daily doings of life.

Bread for the World is, I'm convinced, an instrument of the Lord's peace. Bread for the World raises a prophetic voice of justice speaking to power. Bread for the World is working to reduce the barriers to the coming of the promised kingdom—a kingdom of love, justice, and peace—which remains near, but not yet grasped.

We know that "whoever gives even a cup of cold water to one of these" can look forward to a reward. We keep in touch with the poor by offering cups of water. But more important, we do what we can to apply intellect and political will to eradicate the causes of the hunger that is killing some and stunting the growth of others of our brothers and sisters in the human community.

Unless you are content simply to blame the victim, you have to look around for what might be causing the physical hunger and emotional weariness of those who suffer in our world. You have to try to identify the source of the burdens that are crushing the powerless. If the causes remain unattended, the weariness will persist, the hunger will kill, and the burdens will just grow heavier for those waiting to die.

PRAYER FOR THE HUNGRY

The poor can't count on miracles. The hungry cannot eat promises. It is unlikely that angels will appear on the scene to ease their burdens. Humans helping humans is the way to go. Not the only way to go, say those who believe that miracles are indeed possible. But humans helping humans is a realistic way to go, given the fact that the "miracles" that happen in communities of good and faithful people seem to take a little longer these days.

Where better to begin working for a better world than by attending to hunger, the most urgent form of poverty? How better to address the challenge than by making a commitment to eliminating hunger through advocacy at those human, political decision points where the vulnerable poor can be helped or hurt. Meanwhile, don't forget to pray for those who have no idea where their next meal is coming from, and pray too for those who will have a meal, but not nearly enough to keep them going in the kind of life that we just take for granted.

> Lord, I'm not hungry in a literal, physical sense, but
>   I want to hunger for justice,
>   and I want to let that hunger drive me to do
>   something about injustice.
> Widespread hunger is evidence of injustice in the
>   world that I inhabit.
> Move me, Lord, to do something about it.
> Nudge me in the direction of the needy.

> Not that I'm asking to have my life turned around;
>   just let me make room in my day for doing
>   something—anything—to help,
>   and let me start by helping the hungry poor,
>   and let me begin right here with this prayer.
> Help the hungry poor, Lord; you know them and
>   love them.
> Do away with hunger in our world, Lord; it is an evil
>   that you despise.
> Root out the causes of hunger; banish them forever.
> As I pray, I find myself squirming, Lord.
> I'm skipping a few steps, I know; quite a few.
> I can almost hear you saying to me that you have
>   given me the
>   hands, heart, mind, and resources that,
>   in combination with the hands, hearts, minds, and
>   resources of others,
>   other persons and other nations,
>   can solve the problem of hunger in our world.
> Why don't I use what I have to do what I can?
> Help me figure out an honest answer to that question,
>   Lord,
>   and maybe things will change.

That's the founding vision and spirituality of Bread for the World. The mission is being sustained by Art Simon's successor, David Beckmann, also a Lutheran pastor, who is an economist who used to work at the World Bank. David has been BFW's president since 1991.

World Bank president James Wolfensohn spoke at the BFW's thirtieth birthday celebration in Washington, DC, June 21, 2004 at the National Press Club. He used the word *stellar* to describe David Beckmann and he went on to offer words of encouragement for this faith-based movement.

Wolfensohn complimented BFW by saying, "You don't just go and lobby; you lobby intelligently." The "key issue" of our time, he said, is "poverty and social justice." "If you want peace and stability, you have to look at the issues that drive instability.

You in Bread for the World understand the issues. It is important to follow up and that's what you do. There's a real need in the development business to get back to religion and faith, that's where you began and where you are today."

The BFW reading materials explain that the human family is a global family, but that the world is becoming more unbalanced, with one billion people in the rich countries holding 80 percent of the income, and five billion persons in poor countries holding 20 percent. Inequalities are evident within all countries.

It is "hugely important," said Mr. Wolfensohn, "that you BFW members be successful in your lobbying. You are doing it because it is right. You can measure your effectiveness in human lives, in human dignity, and in social justice."

This organization always works at the national level in coalition with other faith-based advocacy groups. BFW itself can take credit for increasing annual funding for effective poverty-focused programs by an average of $1 billion in 2001, 2002, and 2003. This amounts to about $20,000 per each BFW member. More good results have been achieved since then.

Bread for the World adopted a "Three-Year Plan, 2004–2006," premised on the fact that our nation and the world have the resources *and* the know-how required to end hunger. What then are the priorities for 2004–2006?

BFW is focusing on (1) legislative victories; (2) financial resources or capacity building for the organization itself; and (3) the "Alliance to End Hunger," which is a lead strategy for building the larger movement against hunger.

BFW members hear regularly about the legislative initiatives. In 2004, BFW's annual "Offering of Letters" focused on getting Congress and the president to live up to their promises to provide funding for the new MCA (the Millennium Challenge Account—the U.S. commitment to work with other nations of the world to achieve "Millenium Development Goals") and initiatives to address the HIV-AIDS pandemic in poor countries. The movement's legislative advocacy work fended off efforts to cut back on nutrition and other anti-poverty programs at home and abroad. BFW will be speaking out against more tax cuts for the wealthy as it continues to stress the importance of jobs, earned income, and educational opportunity for the poor.

Capacity building for the organization means raising more people and money, i.e., more members and more outright contributions, to enable the movement to become correspondingly more effective in its advocacy work. A new long-term program of outreach to Latinos was also recently initiated.

The "Alliance to End Hunger" is an exercise in movement building. While maintaining its grounding in Christian faith, BFW wants to enlist large secular organizations to help build political commitment toward the goal of ending hunger.

I shall end by simply quoting the closing paragraph in BFW's seven-page "Three-Year Plan, 2004–2006."

> God has made it possible to end widespread hunger in our country and around the world, so that is Bread for the World's goal. There are political and economic reasons to be discouraged. But as people of resurrection faith, we look to the Lord to act on behalf of the millions of hungry families who cry out for help. We will do our part and, like the people of Israel after crossing the Red Sea, we will remember to praise God for the great liberation we hope to experience.

11

Geno Baroni

In Washington, DC in October 2005, there was a two-day Forum on Public Morality sponsored by the Milton S. Eisenhower Foundation to celebrate what would have been the seventy-fifth birthday of the late Geno Baroni.

It was hard for me to believe, when I received an invitation to present a paper at that forum, that twenty-one years had passed since the death from cancer, at age fifty-three, of Monsignor Geno Baroni on August 27, 1984. It is even harder to have to acknowledge that, for the most part, American social activists have forgotten who he was. Hence the importance, in my mind, of a symposium of celebration and remembrance.

I borrowed a Baroni saying for the title of my (2005) paper: "Action Follows Teaching by Way of Experience," and I added this subtitle: "The Genius of Geno Baroni." It was my hope that the papers delivered during those two days would find their way into print (proceedings have been published) for distribution to a wide audience of thinkers and doers who, in their own unpredictable ways, will bring the Baroni spirit to bear on the effort to find solutions to contemporary social problems.

We simply cannot afford to forget Geno Baroni, the Washington, DC priest and civil rights activist in the sixties; an ethnic neighborhood organizer in the seventies; and, after advising candidate Jimmy Carter in the presidential campaign of 1976, an Assistant Secretary of Housing and Urban Development in the Carter Administration.

Geno Baroni had deep confidence in the wisdom of ordinary people. He valued institutions but worked to hold them accountable, accessible, and responsive to ordinary people. He always looked for ways to establish linkages, to form connections. He thought public policy should be good news for the poor. In the Baroni perspective, "policy is people." His aim was to make the personal political; he would move from home, to neighborhood, to City Hall, and on up the line. The neighborhood- or community-organizer's task is to help people politicize their own good instincts. In addition, Baroni awakened in the hearts of countless talented and generous people a response, translated into career commitments, to the imperative of working for social justice.

Baroni was a complicated genius who did things viscerally, not intellectually. He was not a linear thinker. He moved in patterns rather than in straight lines. He worked the phones, not the typewriter. He had really only one speech; it personalized and interpreted what was known in the seventies as the "white ethnic movement." The basic speech was never written down until after his death when Larry O'Rourke (1991) produced his book, *Geno*, and in it reconstructed The Speech in a chapter titled "Geno's Parables."

THE BARONI PRINCIPLES

I've often wished that we had some Baroni Centers around the country that would train social activists in the Baroni method shaped by what I like to think of as the Baroni principles. If that day ever comes, here are some of Geno's principles that will find their way into the curriculum:

- The role of the Church in social action is to help convene people.
- The organizer has to get ordinary people in touch with their roots, their heritage, their best.
- The organizer has to have deep respect for the ordinary in ordinary people.
- The organizer has to give ordinary people hope.

- The way to break down walls is to go around them by building bridges, forming coalitions, forging bonds.
- Work from idea, to committee, to coalition.
- If you want to save the city, and the country, and the world, you have to start in the neighborhood where people live.
- Neighborhood survival means parish survival; parish survival means neighborhood survival.
- Apathy and violence are cousins coming from the same font—despair. When there is no way out—lack of opportunity, growing frustration, and despair—there is a new kind of psychological poverty that leads to continued apathy and despair.
- Values are at the core of any organizing effort. Take care then to respond to people's deepest hopes and aspirations.
- Never rent a hall you can't fill.
- It is easier to obtain forgiveness than to get permission.
- When you make a mistake, admit it; then pick up the pieces and move on.

Today's troubled Catholic Church in America would do well to incorporate a few Baroni principles into its renewal-and-repair strategies. As Geno used to say, "Action follows teaching by way of experience." We have to respect and learn from all experience, good and bad, pleasant and painful.

On a national scale, the United States of America, through its elected and appointed government officials at all levels, as well as through its leaders in the business and not-for-profit voluntary sector would do well to revive and apply the Baroni principles to contemporary problems.

The Eisenhower Foundation symposium focused on public morality. Given that emphasis, I decided to first establish an unlikely partnership between John Courtney Murray, who fashioned an American public theology, and Geno Baroni, who was never accused of being an intellectual, but fashioned his own American public morality.

Murray the Catholic intellectual; Baroni the Catholic social activist. Murray, the principal architect of the Second Vatican Council's Declaration on Religious Freedom; Baroni the practical mechanic who assembled all the parts of a public morality in a toolkit I'll call The Speech, which Larry O'Rourke has packaged for posterity in his very valuable book.

In an article titled "Citizen Murray," Leon Hooper, S.J. (1995) writes that Father Murray pointed out that Pope John XXIII had "listened while the theologians [who gathered in Rome as consultants to the Fathers of the Second Vatican Council] freely talked, and had an even keener ear for the voice of the simple faithful." Pointing out that Pope John XXIII encouraged the raising of new questions that were "both theological and pastoral—even political," Murray said that "the symbol of him [Pope John] might well be the question mark—surely a unique symbol for a pope."

Murray himself became a listener. He employed the language of natural law—not theological language and categories that could prove to be divisive in pre-ecumenical America—to encourage religious intellectuals to emerge from their respective ghettos to talk to one another about human dignity and human freedom. As Hooper points out, the Church in which Murray grew up and received his theological training "insisted that the elites impose religious and moral demands on the masses for their own protection. By church law, the elites were to be intolerant of differing voices, particularly if those voices belonged to the people at large." Murray, according to Hooper, "countered with what he called a 'great act of faith' in the moral possibilities of the people, an idea he developed within the Anglo-American political tradition."

As a student of the development of Murray's thought, Leon Hooper observes, "Given the complexity of modern social life, the silencing of voices that might have something to contribute to our common life is social suicide." "If Murray taught us anything," says Hooper, "it was to not fear those voices, for in them a dynamic, creative God is to be found." To this, of course, Citizen Baroni would add a warm Amen.

CITIZEN BARONI

Citizen Baroni speaks to us in Larry O'Rourke's chapter fifteen, titled "Geno's Parables." There, as I mentioned earlier, you will find The Speech. If you read it, you'll notice that the question mark would be an apt symbol for Baroni; The Speech is sprinkled with question marks. Listen for a moment: "Why can't we have a multi-diverse, a pluralistic, value system way of life and respect these life systems [of minority communities] and stop being so competitive and develop a mutual interdependence? Can we do it? Is that the only option to conflict and chaos? Can we find a new identity? Can we find a new national purpose? Can we create a society that meets the human needs of the poor, which is always a test of standards?"

The planners of the symposium honoring Baroni's memory raised more than a few questions for the consideration of those preparing papers for delivery there. For example, "How would Geno Baroni frame the role of religion in 2005 to reinforce a progressive agenda?" Again, since he "viewed the federal budget as a moral document and told us that 'every economic and social issue is a moral issue,' would not Geno therefore possibly have framed solutions more in terms of public morality than in terms of faith-based initiatives?" Perhaps he would. Certainly he would be emphasizing the moral dimension—the public morality issue—but he might in his canny practical way see *faith-based* as a category that's been out there during the George W. Bush presidency, waiting to be used for good on-the-ground purposes.

No one knew better than Geno that politics is the art of compromise. Some religious people have been and remain skeptical about the workability of President Bush's faith-based initiatives since they were first proposed. Some fear that religious principle will be compromised in the process. In my view, that need never happen.

Others fear that the establishment clause or better, the *non-establishment* clause) of the First Amendment to our Constitution will be violated if government gives money to religiously motivated organizations to assist them in rendering social services to the needy. This, in my view, is not a well-grounded fear. Roman Catholicism will not become the established religion of the United States if the federal government funnels federal dollars through Catholic Charities USA in an effort to help the hungry and homeless. Nor will any other denomination become established as a controlling religious entity just because that denomination's social service arm is strengthened by an infusion of federal funding.

NO SEPARATION OF CHURCH AND SOCIETY

There is no separation of church and society in the United States, nor was such a separation ever intended by our founding fathers. Even though we speak of the separation of church and state, the *wall* of separation is a misleading metaphor that appears nowhere in the Constitution. When permitted to function as a wall separating government from any involvement at all with private, faith-based, religiously motivated organizations, the First Amendment is being both misunderstood and misapplied.

There is a time-honored, quite conservative principle in the tradition of Catholic social teaching that should be brought into play in the public debate as to whether government money can or should be channeled into religious charities. This principle is intended to keep government in its proper place, active or inactive depending on the circumstances. It is known as the principle of *subsidiarity*. It applies to any form of organization, not just government. In essence, it states that no decisions or actions should be taken at a higher level of organization that can be taken as efficiently and effectively at a lower level—closer to the people that will be affected, closer to the ground. The application of this principle depends on circumstances. It forecloses on big government in cases where government would be walking over lower-level decision-makers to get good things done. Conversely, it would require and fully justify government action in circumstances where programs good for the people should be in place but the resources of lower-level organizations fall far short of the need and only government is big enough to make up the difference. I think Geno Baroni would be pleased to see the principle of subsidiarity included in any set of Baroni principles!

The federal government can fund the Salvation Army's coffee and blankets, but not its hymnbooks. We're not talking about Lutheran sandwiches or Baptist bandages when we speak of religiously based aid to the poor. We are, indeed, talking about poor people and how society might reach out to them. If faith-related hands are there right now, at the ready, so to speak, why not give them the wherewithal to extend themselves in the direction of urgent human need? In examining the list of possible reasons, don't fail to consider religious discrimination. It is easier to invoke the Constitution than to admit to anti-(fill in the blank) prejudice whenever you notice a religion or religious organization that is doing good (not well) and could be doing more (not better), and would be doing more if those who distrust or discriminate against that religion were not so intent on blocking access to the federal faucets.

We didn't hear much about the poor in the first seven years of the Clinton presidency. In the George W. Bush presidency we heard a lot about meeting the needs of the poor at one remove from government, i.e., through non-governmental agencies that happen to be faith-based and are still in close touch with the needy. They know how to reach the poor. The White House Office of Faith-Based and Community Initiatives was there to work with them. Has anyone heard the poor say they didn't want to see this happen?

THE UNEASY INTERSECTION

We know, of course, that religion can be co-opted for partisan political purposes. You have to wonder, for instance, about Justice Sunday on April 24, 2005 when a televised simulcast to churches to rally religious conservatives who wanted to deny Democrats the ability to mount a filibuster barring votes on President Bush's judicial nominees, prompted *Business Week* to editorialize: "The rancor surrounding the event has become so unseemly that it raises a vital question: After a quarter-century of arguing about the growing impact of religion on American politics, could this intermarriage with politics inadvertently take its toll on religion?.... The religious community should remain involved; that's the right and responsibility of every American. But what makes religion so potent is its ability to cross divisions like racial, regional, and party, lines. So when religion is used in the exclusionary manner we're increasingly seeing in some political quarters, it just seems like divide-and-conquer politics as usual."

Geno Baroni would indeed be wary of all that, but wise enough to work his way through it for the advantage of the poor and powerless. Remember, he was convinced that action follows teaching by way of experience. There has always been an uneasy intersection between religion and politics in America. But look at the trophies of success religion helped to win in the abolition movement, and in the civil rights and anti-war movements. What might religion be doing today in the matter of minimum wage, universal health insurance, immigration reform and so many other issues that come to the mind of anyone who is the least bit concerned for the common good.

In the Baroni spirit of respect for the values and concerns of the little people, I think we should be asking them—the little people—what they need for their fair share of participation in the good life. Hurricane Katrina brought the voices of many of them to the attention of the nation by means of radio and television. Those voices spoke of immediate urgent needs; the lives behind those voices told stories of dreams long deferred, justice long denied.

I think Baroni would be all over the faith-based initiators of help for poor and homeless people—Katrina evacuees and others like them—to use the existing faith-related institutional bases to connect federal relief with those most in need. I think Baroni would be all over FEMA (Federal Emergency Management Administration) and other governmental entities—local, state, and federal—to demand more effective communication, more competent management, and improved coordination of the public response to need in time of crisis. And it is not too much of a stretch of my imagination to think of Geno Baroni making these demands in a vocabulary of public morality.

WE HOLD THESE TRUTHS

Recall that John Courtney Murray constructed moral arguments in the language of the natural law. He identified that language in the vocabulary of our founders and framers—"We hold these truths to be self-evident." Why self-evident? Because they were available to human reason unaided by divine revelation. As Leon Hooper states it, natural law "is based on the moral law that God instilled in human nature at creation, rather than on the law given to the Church in the dying and rising of Jesus. As such, it is available to all people of good will, regardless of their faith." From this starting point, Murray developed an American public theology. Baroni's American public morality would not be articulated in learned tomes. If he were around today, he would be exhibiting it in his personalized, faith-based social activism. He would use the tools and strategies of community organizing, focusing on the issues of immediate concern to the people in the neighborhoods he would be fighting to preserve.

Would abortion be one of those issues? Probably not. It would surely surface in the political campaigns waged by those seeking elective office in order to serve the needs of the little people (as it did in the Carter campaign), but it would not be a little people's issue. Baroni would play it down as a campaign issue while trying to figure out a way to prevent it from becoming destructive of the unity needed to move a progressive social agenda, geared directly to the needs of the little people, forward. If he developed a public morality vocabulary, as Murray developed a public theology vocabulary, the door would be open to the argument that abortion is not really, and certainly not exclusively, a Catholic issue. He would argue that Catholic politicians should not be condemned, and certainly not denied access to the Eucharist, because of votes that fall short of the pro-life standards of the Catholic hierarchy.

He would find helpful in making his argument the words of the late Catholic theologian Monika Hellwig, who said in a 2004 all-day forum on abortion and politics at the National Press Club: "The issue of abortion is not a Catholic issue, it's a human issue. It's an issue which in our traditional understanding is supposed to be discussed at the level of natural law, at the level of the public square, at the level of enlisting the reflection of all people of good will and enlisting their reflection in a sustained, coherent argument about the case." Dr. Hellwig reminded those who called for the bishops to deny Communion to Catholics who vote against legal restrictions on abortion, that they were reinforcing the widespread misperception that abortion is just a Catholic issue, not a public issue for all Americans to confront.

I'm confident that Baroni would oppose abortion under any circumstances, but would be willing to yield some ground to those who conscientiously disagree, in the hope that the compromise—not on principle but on policy—would mean a significant reduction in abortions in America. What would such a compromise involve? Narrowing the range of legally permissible abortion to cases of rape, incest, or the life of the mother, and decriminalizing the offense.

Narrowing the range of permissibility would bring the matter closer to what I believe (and I suspect Baroni would agree) is the national consensus on protection of unborn human life. But just raising this question invites strong opposition from defenders of a woman's unrestricted right to choose to terminate the life within her womb at any stage of the pregnancy. I think Geno would want to move away from that discussion and talk about housing, neighborhoods, homelessness, capital punishment, the condition of prisons, the medically uninsured, the uneducated and unemployed. He would want to talk about those locked in low levels of literacy, and the victims of drug addiction. He would want to talk about getting out of Iraq and he would certainly want to talk about the priorities (as well as the values) embodied in our federal budget.

I've often remarked that Geno Baroni never took the American automobile fully into account. He did not reflect on the role of the automobile in destroying old neighborhoods (and this in two ways—by overloading the narrow streets of existing neighborhoods with parked and abandoned cars, and by providing easy access out of the city into the suburbs without breaking the link to city-based employment). Nor did he appear to understand how the automobile became a substitute source of power, prestige, and social mobility for poor people who could have earned these advances the hard way through education, apprenticeship, and discipline—had the reinforcing social structure been in place in the old neighborhoods to sustain them.

Perhaps that's an agenda to be taken up when Baroni admirers gather in 2030 for another forum, that one marking the one hundredth anniversary of his birth.

12

■

Social Justice Education

I'm often asked to speak abut justice to a variety of audiences and I usually approach the topic by saying that there is an age-old pedagogical debate that I'll identify but not attempt to resolve. One way of framing the issue in this debate is to ask a fundamental question. Do you *think* your way into new ways of acting, or *act* your way into new ways of thinking?

That question reaches all the way back to Plato and Aristotle, where you would find Plato tilting toward thinking one's way into new ways of acting, and Aristotle displaying a bias toward acting one's way into new ways of thinking.

If you were to pose the question of how best to come to an understanding of justice in these terms, you would find some educators convinced that once a clear idea of justice is grasped, just actions will follow. Plato would endorse that approach. Others, under the influence of an Aristotelian tradition, would suggest that the experience of justice, or better for pedagogical purposes, the experience of injustice, is the best way to dispose the mind to grasp an understanding of the meaning of justice.

Pay your tuition, so to speak, and take your choice.

Those paying tuition for formal education in a physical science will soon notice that both approaches are employed on the road to understanding. Next to the lecture hall is a laboratory. Listen to the lecture, take your notes, read the text, and then go to the lab to put the theory into practice.

Understanding awaits the inquiring mind in either venue; it is usually produced by a convergence of the two learning environments on the one inquiring mind.

The think-your-way versus the act-your-way approach to an understanding of justice is always a timely question for educators. "The trouble with our world," someone once observed, "is that the people who do all the acting never think, and the people who do all the thinking never act." If something is going to be done to correct present (and prevent future) injustices, education for justice will have to produce principled actors and engaged thinkers. Where, however, is the laboratory for a student trying to gain an understanding of the meaning of justice? Creative pedagogy has to provide both instruction and age-appropriate "labs" that will help a student better understand justice.

IDEAS AND IMAGES

Educators are in the idea industry; they are in the business of stimulating and communicating understanding. The focus of my approach here will be on the educational challenge of communicating an understanding of justice. I treat the topic by considering both ideas and images of justice, and offering along the way a few practical suggestions related to justice education.

Ideas of justice are both familiar and plentiful: treating equals equally; giving to each person his or her due; being fair. The great tradition of Catholic social teaching provides additional ideas of justice in the form of principles. It is important to notice that principles are ideas in need of legs; they are articulated in order to prompt activity; they are intended to lead to something.

As I mentioned in chapter two, I (1998) published an article in *America* under the title "Ten Building Blocks of Catholic Social Teaching." The editors substituted *building blocks* for the word *principles* that appeared in my original title in order to strengthen the point the article makes, namely, that these principles have to be put to work in the construction of a just society. I listed ten principles, ten ideas that have to be grasped and then put to work. These ideas are as follows: the primacy of human dignity, respect for human life, association, participation, preferential protection for the poor and vulnerable, solidarity, stewardship, subsidiarity, human equality, and the principle of the common good. These principles have a history; they embody layers of meaning. They have to be understood and internalized—accepted and made one's own.

Images help this process along. There is, for instance, the image the prophet Amos employed to communicate the idea of justice. Recall that prophets are not those who, as the popular imagination portrays them, predict the future. Old Testament prophets like Amos are those who point to the present injustice and warn that if corrective action is not taken, dire consequences will follow. Since, more often than not, appropriate action was not taken and the consequences followed, the prophet became known as one who foretold the future (the dire consequences). But the key role of the prophet is being God's voice in denouncing an evil and calling for remedial action, and being God's finger in pointing to an existing injustice. Listen then to the prophet Amos (7:7–9): "Then the Lord God showed me this: he was standing by a wall, plummet in hand. The Lord asked me, 'What do you see, Amos?' And when I answered, 'A plummet,' the Lord said: 'See, I will lay the plummet in the midst of my people Israel; I will forgive them no longer. The high places of Isaac shall be laid waste, and the sanctuaries of Israel made desolate; I will attack the house of Jeroboam with the sword.'"

This is the famous image of the plumb bob. You sometimes see them in little holsters on the hips of surveyors. Although new technology means that they are used less frequently now, they are employed by surveyors in staking out the lines and boundaries of new roads and other construction projects. The plummet—or, as we call it today, the plumb bob—drops directly down from the surveyor's fingers; it is a pointed, cone-shaped metal weight that seeks the earth's center. The string from the plumb bob to the fingers holding it creates a vertical line—a plumb line—to be seen in the cross hairs of the surveyor's instrument, the transit.

Israel is going to be measured for its uprightness, its justice, says the Lord, through the voice of Amos. If the nation is not upright, if it is *out of plumb*, as builders would say, it will surely collapse. Think for a moment of how we borrow from the vocabulary of the building trades to communicate an idea of justice—*on the level, fair and square, up and up, four square*. An unjust society will fall just as surely as will a wall under construction that is not straight, that is, out of plumb. (And by extension, we have the familiar exhortation, usually from a father to a son, "Straighten up and fly right! Or else!!")

Another useful image is water. Recall that water always seeks its own level. And think of the straightforwardness, the directness, of a waterfall. Listen again to Amos (5:24): "Let justice surge [roll down] like water, and goodness like an unfailing stream."

THE SCALES OF JUSTICE

By far the best image of justice for purposes of communicating an understanding of justice is, in my opinion, the familiar scales of justice, the ubiquitous image of two trays in balance on a scale. Recall how Justice is represented in the statue of a woman, tall and strong, a blindfold over her eyes, her arm extended straight in front of her, her right hand holding the scales. The blindfold signals the court's impartiality to either side in a dispute. When the scales are even, justice prevails. When an unfair advantage is taken, it shows as an unfair gain taken at the expense of the other's loss. Compensatory action (*pensa* is the Latin word for weights) is called for; the weights must be redistributed so as to bring the trays back into balance—into a state of justice. You see the scales of justice as insignia on lawyers' cuff links, tie clips, and other jewelry... on desk ornaments, wall hangings, and bookends.

Apply the image of the scales of justice for purposes of social analysis. If I pick your pocket (a simple one-on-one example of injustice), my gain is taken at the expense of your loss. To make things right again, I've got to get that wallet back where it belongs—on your tray. Now think of other imbalances from the perspective of social justice, still employing the framework of the scales of justice. Look at the differences in life expectancy between African American children and their European American contemporaries. Compare educational attainments or income distributions between selected groups. Think of compensation received in the workplace by men and women doing essentially the same work. Consider daily caloric intake in the developed over against the less developed economies of the world. Look at the balance (or imbalance) of trade between rich nations and poor.

In every case the question is the same. *Is one tray's favored weight taken at the expense of deprivation on the other tray?* There must, of course, be some relatedness if the analysis is to conclude that corrective action is required in the name of justice. The relatedness between a pickpocket and his or her victim is clear. Not so clear is the relationship between the advantaged and disadvantaged groups in the other comparisons I just made. To the extent that there is an identifiable relationship between the two, then you can begin to look for evidence that one side's gain has indeed been taken (and is still being enjoyed) because of the other side's loss. There is a clear causal connection and justice calls for remedial action. It might be established, for instance, that the imbalance is the result of prejudice, exploitation, greed, or abuse of power.

Where imbalance is evident, but a relationship is not obvious and a causal relationship cannot be established, then charity, compassion, the common good, a commitment to solidarity, and social responsibility will call for compensatory action that strict justice might not be able to compel. At times, appeal has to be made to our sense of humanity if action is to be taken to correct inhumane conditions or clear wrongs that have ambiguous or even contested social origins. The problem will not go away on its own. Even if the accusing finger can find no clear target, an honest social conscience will accept the verdict Rabbi Abraham Joshua Heschel once rendered in the face of massive social injustice, "Some are guilty; all are responsible." Widespread acceptance of that verdict means that some corrective action will certainly follow.

SUBSIDIARITY

Another idea of justice is embodied in the principle of subsidiarity; I find a useful image to explain this notion in five bronze figures that are part of the seven-acre, open-air memorial to Franklin Delano Roosevelt near the Tidal Basin in Washington, DC. The principle of subsidiarity states simply that no decisions or action should be taken at a higher level of organization (government being the primary reference point here) that can be taken as effectively and efficiently at a lower level of organization. FDR was first elected to the presidency in 1932, in the depths of the Great Depression. Something simply had to be done about massive poverty and unemployment in this nation. Could the private sector do it? Or, was the job so big that only government—the federal government—had to act? Roosevelt decided that only the government was up to the challenge so he led a vigorous program of federal initiatives.

The five bronze figures of dejected men, with overcoat collars turned up and hat brims pulled down, are lined up against a wall awaiting the opening of a soup-kitchen door in the second "room" of the FDR Memorial that represents the second term of the Roosevelt presidency. The New Deal was underway. A federal Social Security program had been enacted to address the monumental challenge of doing something to meet the needs of "one third of a nation" that the moving Roosevelt Second Inaugural rhetoric—inscribed on the wall of this section of the FDR Memorial—described as "ill-housed, ill-clad, ill-nourished." The task was too large for the private sector; only the federal government had the resources for effective and efficient action.

Every spring, thousands of school children visit Washington to see the federal buildings, monuments, and memorials. Platoons of youngsters descend on the FDR Memorial; invariably the kids slot themselves in between the bronze figures and have souvenir snapshots taken. Unaided, they are quite unlikely to realize that the bronze figures represent their grandfathers or great grandfathers. These children of prosperity with their long life expectancy, good health, educational advantages, and so much more, have to be helped to understand that something extraordinary happened in America in the thirties. Their visit to Washington can be a teaching moment to learn something about the principle of subsidiarity and its relationship to significant social problems.

COMMON GOOD

Another justice-related idea is embodied in the principle of the common good. In its "Pastoral Constitution on The Church in the Modern World" (No. 26), the Second Vatican Council described the common good as "the sum of those conditions of social life which allow social groups and their individual members relatively thorough and ready access to their own fulfillment." It is not the sum of all the individual goods, nor is it a utilitarian kind of greatest good for the greatest number of people. It involves rather a conscious sense of respect for all persons, an acknowledgment of the basic human dignity of everyone, and a commitment to work for the promotion of conditions in society that encourage the development of each person's human potential. This idea is related to the principle of solidarity, the notion that we are, by virtue of our common human nature, connected to one another, part of the one human family. The principle of solidarity functions as a moral category that leads to choices that will promote and protect the common good. We are, indeed, our brothers' and sisters' keepers and we are obligated to act accordingly. The fact that an estimated forty-four million Americans are currently not covered by any form of health insurance is an issue to be considered as an assault on the common good, a blow to our sense of solidarity.

An image that helps the individual self-interested mind wrap itself around the notions of solidarity and common good is the image of the old-fashioned inner tube and a rubber tire. The wholeness and roundness of the tire suggests the oneness of society. The inner tube's potential for wear and tear—the potential for a blowout that can flatten the entire tire—serves to remind us that it is in the interest of the whole tire that attention be paid to a small section in need of a plug or patch. Promotion of the common good protects the ultimate good of the individual.

PREFERENCE FOR THE POOR

Another social justice idea is the principle of a preferential option—or preferential protection—for the poor. Imagine a parent walking on the sidewalk between a twelve-year-old and a frisky three-year-old child. The toddler breaks away and runs out into the street in the path of oncoming traffic. The parent naturally and without hesitation runs out to protect the vulnerable child, leaving the twelve-year-old to fend for him- or herself in the relative security of the sidewalk. That is what I call preferential protection. It is what the Church asks of us in calling for a preferential love of the poor. Those who find this principle difficult to accept might be helped by the reassuring words of Pope John Paul II, who explained in a talk entitled, "Ecclesia in America," given in Mexico City on January 22, 1999: "Love for the poor must be preferential, but not exclusive." The more fortunate among us have to be reminded from time to time that just because we happen not to be poor is no reason at all to conclude that we are not the constant objects of God's unfailing love.

Other images that help believers gain an understanding of their societal obligations under the principles of fairness, solidarity, participation, association, and the common good are the familiar ones of a loaf of bread and a flowing river.

A two-word Latin phrase, *cum pane*, which means *with bread*, calls attention to what Christians do in the Eucharistic assembly where they gather to remember the Lord in the breaking of the bread. Their faith requires them to be bread breakers. Like the bread they break, they too—living as they do under the new commandment of love (John 15:12)—should be willing to break themselves open in loving service to others. At the Last Supper on the night before he died, Christ said, in effect, this is how I want you to remember me, as bread broken and passed around for the nourishment of others, as a cup poured out in selfless service. It is interesting to note that those same two words—cum pane—are the etymological basis for the English word *company*, the place where people ordinarily go to work. Eucharistic bread breakers—sharers in the *com-panionship* of the Lord's Table—are expected to bring the spirit of companionship to their respective workplaces, to the companies that employ them and to their companions on the job.

The river metaphor provides another image that works well to suggest that the goods of God's creation are intended for the use of all. They flow as a river through all the nations that are lined up, so to speak, on the river's banks. What are we to think of a situation where one nation, because of cunning, deceit, conquest, or simple good fortune, enjoys a favorable upstream location and uses that advantage to divert an unusually large share of the flow (the wealth) for its own national purposes? Is that fair? If not, what might (must?) be done to even up the distribution? Do the less favored nations and tribes along the banks have a word in deciding how the wealth is to be distributed? (Is it any wonder, by the way, that the poorer nations might not have affection and regard for the dominant, powerful, arrogant, and self-aggrandizing nations located upstream?)

FACES AND PHRASES

Ideas and images are necessary—but are not in themselves sufficient—helps in communicating an understanding of justice. Faces and sayings are also needed. Put the face of Dorothy Day, the pacifist founder of the Catholic Worker movement, in this picture. I once heard her describe her two basic operating principles—personal guidelines for all her choices—this way: "Always be on the side of the poor. Always be on the side of peace." No matter what the issue happened to be, she filtered it through those twin convictions before making her decision.

Cesar Chavez is another face that belongs here. An advocate for justice, specifically for the rights of powerless and unrepresented farm workers, Chavez was committed to nonviolence in the pursuit of social change.

Rosa Parks belongs in this picture. Her decision to *sit* for human dignity triggered the Montgomery bus boycott and gradually brought a reluctant nation to *stand up* for civil rights. The face of the Reverend Dr. Martin Luther King, Jr. comes to mind, of course, with any mention of civil rights.

The face of Cardinal Joseph Bernardin will serve to recall his well-reasoned argument for a consistent ethic of life. Part of that consistent ethic is the consideration of capital punishment, which fits into the picture right there along with the issues of abortion, euthanasia, and nuclear war. Mention of capital punishment brings to mind the face of Sister Helen Prejean, whose (1997) book *Dead Man Walking* became the film that brought a nation to reflect again on the fairness of the death penalty as the twentieth century came to a close.

The face of Pope John Paul II belongs in this picture; with it, you will have to make room for an array of urgent and vexing social justice issues covering a broader range than any papal pen ever before addressed.

Mother Teresa of Calcutta has a special place in this picture even though her strong suit was not the reform of social structures. She put a compelling face on the preferential option for the poor and raised the standard of Christian compassion for the dying destitute.

More faces are out there in the world and in the history books. Some faces are to be found in good literature—Huck Finn, to mention only one (whom I like to mention often!), put a face on integrity, authenticity, and incorruptibility. Recall the fix he found himself in. He was helping Jim, a runaway slave, to gain his freedom. The law said Jim was property; he belonged to Miss Watson. According to the law, Huck was stealing, taking something that didn't belong to him. In befriending a black man and in treating him as an equal, Huck was acting contrary to both law and custom. Huck had been taught that Jim was not his equal. Huck had internalized the dominant public opinion about the institution of slavery—it was not only acceptable but the quite proper way of doing things. But he began to believe that slavery was wrong; he felt stirrings in himself that prompted him to reject a law that he knew, deep down, to be unjust and immoral. But it wasn't easy. Listen to him agonize: "The more I studied about this the more my conscience went to grinding me, and the more wicked and lowdown and ornery I got to feeling.... It made me shiver.... I was a-trembling, because I'd got to decide, forever, betwixt two things, and I knowed it. I studied a minute, sort of holding my breath, and then says to myself: 'All right then, I'll go to hell.' "

And that, as I've often said, marked a break for Huck from both law and religion insofar as they supported the institution of slavery that he, in his heart of hearts, knew to be plain wrong. "It was awful thoughts and awful words," Huck adds, "but they were said. And I let them stay said; and never thought no more about reforming."

Better, perhaps, if he had said, "never thought no more about *conforming*"—to unjust laws, to inhuman institutions, to unexamined and unfair social conventions.

Many more faces—real-world and fictional—are there to be put on the principles for the purpose of making those principles more accessible to the inquiring mind.

PRACTICAL CONSIDERATIONS

Now for a few practical suggestions. First, since so much of the terrain to be covered in coming to an understanding of justice relates to the problem of poverty, I offer a simple two-word definition of poverty. Call it *sustained deprivation*. Those two words catch the essence of the meaning of poverty, but they do not say it all. In order to analyze a given situation two questions must be immediately raised: *Deprived of what? Sustained by what or by whom?*

Deprived of income, nutrition, housing, education, healthcare, economic security. Sustained by ignorance, injustice, greed, and abuse of power. Figure it out and then lay out a strategy for remedial action. And for what it's worth (and it should be worth a lot to shore up the sometimes sagging spirits of educators), let me state my personal conviction that it would be difficult to find anyone who is well educated and also involuntarily poor. So, if you want to do something about poverty, see what you can do to make sure that the poor become well educated. Just as Pope Paul VI once remarked that if you want peace, you should work for justice; let me suggest that if you want to eliminate poverty, see what you can do to improve educational attainment.

As a practical matter, justice educators should take care to distinguish ethical justice (giving to each person his or her due) from biblical justice (attending to fidelity—fidelity to our relationships to God, to the people God has placed here with us on earth, and to the care of God's creation). Reason helps us get a grasp on ethical justice; revelation, which presupposes faith, provides the foundation for coming to terms personally and as a faith community with the demands of biblical justice. There will indeed be demands.

Take, for instance, the issue of world hunger. Hunger is a justice issue. One of the best ways, in my experience, of getting in touch with the hunger issue is through Bread for the World, a Christian citizens' lobby mentioned in a previous chapter that has, for more than thirty years, been an effective advocate for the hungry poor by lobbying the U.S. government's legislative and executive branches. Bread for the World's analysis of the issues is always sound; the advocacy is always sane. (Both the lobbying organization, Bread for the World, and its politically neutral educational arm known as the Bread for the World Institute, are located at 50 F Street, NW, Suite 500, Washington, DC 20001; phone 202-639-9400; fax 202-639-9401; e-mail bread@bread.org.)

Another very practical consideration in the matter of education for justice is to urge all students to learn a second language. Spanish is a preferred option for North Americans given the North-South hemispheric issues that have a justice dimension, but any foreign language will do. The second language, aside from giving the students "eyes in the back of their heads," as a character in one of Flannery O'Connor's short stories puts it, will help them realize that they are participants in a global economy and citizens of a very big world.

Educators are faced with the practical challenge of encouraging their students to avoid individualism and become what I call *individuarians*. As I explained in the opening chapter of this book, that word is not yet in the dictionary. It is one I employ to describe men and women who are neither rugged individualists nor ideological communists, even though they are strong-minded, unique individuals. Just as *communitarian* is a label that came into currency to describe a socially responsible, environmentally sensitive, community-minded outlook, individuarian now strikes me as useful in setting a community-minded person apart from the individual of the psychologist and the collectivity of the sociologist. Individuarians are balanced persons willing to live their lives bordered by the personal and the communal; they are individuals in community.

COMMUNITY SERVICE

Community service, in age-appropriate settings, is a great laboratory in which an understanding of justice can be (not necessarily *will be*) gained by students from middle school on up. They call it service learning, but the learning won't happen without on-site supervision and off-site guided reflection on the experience.

James Youniss, of The Catholic University of America, and Miranda Yates, of Brown University, are co-authors (1997, 135) of an outstanding book, *Community Service and Social Responsibility in Youth*. They offer ten ideas that reflect their thesis that "service can provide concrete opportunities for youth to develop an increased understanding of their membership within a societal framework and their responsibility for society's future." All ten ideas touch upon the common themes of engaging youth in society and making service an integral part of personal identity. Service should not be seen by young persons as an isolated experience; it needs to become integrated into their lives. The process is developmental (not surprisingly, the authors are developmental psychologists). Here is a summary of their ten points; the entire book is highly recommended.

1. The quality rather than the quantity of service is the important point. Meaningful service, as opposed to a make-work situation, should include responsibility for decision making; identification and reflection upon one's personal values; working closely with adults; facing new situations; and receiving blame or credit for one's work.

2. The emphasis should be on helping others. Avoid overemphasizing the benefit of the experience to the service provider. Put the emphasis on helping others in order to cultivate in the service provider caring attitudes and a commitment to social justice.
3. The service should be connected to the defining goal or mission of the school.
4. Group action is preferred to individual service. A sense of group awareness is important; collective action thrives on a clearly defined sense of the *we* who do the action.
5. Reflection on the experience is essential. Personal essays and journal-keeping aid reflection; peer discussion groups are important complements to private reflection.
6. Adults who organize the service opportunities and work along with the students provide admirable and imitable examples that the *message* can be *lived*.
7. People who work full time at the service sites "can be models of moral commitment who offer their perspective on social problems and the dynamics of trying to alleviate these problems. While the ability of staff members to be educators may be limited by time and resources, this potential should not be overlooked when service organizers select sites and establish relationships with the staff at these sites."
8. Typically, the mix of participants, site supervisors, service organizers, and recipients of the service will be quite diverse. This can cause discomfort that should be acknowledged because diversity of race, class, and gender can affect the service experience; it is something that should be talked about as part of reflection on the experience.
9. A sense of being part of history should be engendered in the students. This sense enables the service to have a powerful impact on identity development. "Youth become invested in service when they believe that their actions are helping to make history. On the other hand, it is also easy to understand how youth can maintain the disengaged role of voyeur when service is treated as an isolated or decontextualized event."
10. Service helps focus students on their responsibilities rather than on their rights and freedoms.

Again, I refer the reader to Youniss and Yates (1997) for a fuller elaboration of these points. Let me also point interested readers in the direction of my article, "A Religious-Based College and University Perspective," in a collection of essays edited by Thomas Ehrlich (2000, 279–94) in *Civic Responsibility and Higher Education*.

THE QUIET VIRTUES

I conclude with an observation about style. How should students conduct themselves while rendering community service and working for social justice? They should first become acquainted with what St. Paul, writing to the Galatians, lists as the fruit of the Spirit—evidence that the Holy Spirit is present in a person and in that person's work: love, joy, peace, patience, kindness, generosity, faithfulness, gentleness, and self-control (Gal. 5:22). These are all quiet virtues; Paul cites them as evidence that the Holy Spirit is there, active and engaged in the effort. The same Holy Spirit is also there in the noisier virtues of justice, fortitude, advocacy, and prophetic denunciation. But an infrastructure of the quiet virtues, the nine Pauline criteria for the presence of the Spirit, must first be in place to guarantee that it is the Holy Spirit, not the self-love and assertive ego of the advocate, that is making necessary noise on the road to justice. (We'll return to these Pauline principles in chapter fifteen where they will be laid out as an infrastructure for a functioning workplace spirituality.)

To repeat a point made earlier—I don't know anyone who is well educated and also involuntarily poor. So I offer a word of encouragement to educators who see so much poverty on the underside of injustice. Good education for justice is anti-poverty activity. The world moves on words and numbers, on ideas and images. Educators communicate an understanding of (and the ability to manage) all four. Their commitment to education as an instrument of social change puts them in a privileged position that enables them to work (not rest) assured that what they do is helping to build a just society.

13

Wealth and Responsibility

Reflections in chapter twelve on the idea of justice open the door to further reflection on the notion of wealth and its associated responsibilities. What I offer in this short chapter is an interpretive framework for this kind of consideration.

It might be useful at the outset to distinguish wealth from income. Wealth, although it can be lost, suggests stability, while there is a fluidity associated with income. The income stream may flow deep and full, but it moves on through. Unless a significant portion of income is diverted away from current expenditures and saved (held in reserve), it will make no contribution to wealth. Moreover, one can be a recipient of passive income (interest and dividends) as well as an active generator of cold, hard, spendable cash. An "easy come, easy go," cash-in-hand personal situation can produce a "wealthy" lifestyle that comes to a sudden halt when the income stream dries up. The appearance of wealth can be a prelude to poverty, if there has been no accumulation, no stability, no—to employ a theological term—stewardship.

There is, of course, a lot more to wealth than liquid assets held in the form of what we, interestingly enough, call *securities*. Stocks and bonds (financial assets) are an important component of wealth. But so are contracts, real estate holdings (land and improvements), furniture and fixtures, livestock or rolling stock, and indeed what we sometimes refer to as intellectual property (patents and copyrights that have a marketable value).

Just as poverty can be defined as *sustained deprivation*—i.e., deprivation, over time, of health, shelter, education, employment, and income, sustained by social and economic forces some of which might be unjust—so wealth can be thought of as sustained possession—possession over time of the good things, materially speaking, that this world has to offer, sustained by personal choice and an economic system that may or may not be guided by the principles of justice.

So any serious reflection on wealth and responsibility will have to touch upon the notions of both stewardship and justice.

THE REQUIREMENTS OF STEWARDSHIP

A traditional theological understanding of stewardship rests on the first verse of Psalm 24: "The earth is the Lord's, and the fullness thereof." The earth—all of it, and all that it contains—belongs to God. We are users and managers. Stewardship says that we are not owners in any absolute sense. We may indeed have private ownership rights, protected by law, as a means of making possible responsible management of our possessions (representing, as they do, "the fullness thereof"). As stewards, we have to protect, preserve, and provide for future generations, sustainable and life-sustaining grasslands, croplands, woodlands, seas, rivers, and lakes. Stewardship requires us to use the resources beneath the surface of the earth wisely, and to use our intellectual resources in a way that meets the challenge of substitution or replacement for non-renewable natural resources. Natural wealth will not be managed responsibly absent a commitment on the part of all to the common good.

Justice joins stewardship to address the questions of the uses and accumulation of wealth. Are there limits on accumulation? How much is too much? Are there guidelines for responsible use? Yes there are, and they are part of our tradition of Catholic social thought.

Recognizing the imperfections and propensities of our acquisitive human nature, the tradition of Catholic social thought would say to the question of responsible use that ownership of property can be private, but use is common. Genuine need posts a just claim against privately owned but insufficiently used property. Hence a moral limit on ownership—put another way, a moral guideline for responsible ownership—would be the amount of property that an owner might reasonably use. To pile it up, stash it away, or shut it down when genuine need is out there seeking a share not for comfort but for survival, is to violate a principle of justice in the ownership and management of one's possessions. The responsible owner, refusing to be possessed by his or her possessions, will be open to sharing in the face of genuine human need. The irresponsible owner, refusing to share in the face of genuine need, should be targeted for blame and shame (and conversion).

What I'm saying here of individuals is also applicable to corporations and especially to nations. Think, for instance, of the responsibilities of so-called *have* nations over against their *have-not* neighbors on the map of the world relative, say, to hunger. Think also of our individual, corporate, and national responsibility to protect our physical environment.

A *Compendium of the Social Doctrine of the Church* (2005) was published by the Pontifical Council for Justice and Peace. Under *income*, the index lists only two entries: "distribution of income and justice" and "informal economic activities and low incomes." Under *wealth*, however, there are twenty-six items ranging from "Jesus and wealth" to "riches and sharing."

The *Compendium* repeats the tough teaching of early church fathers like Clement of Alexandria, John Chrysostom, Basil the Great, and Gregory the Great and sums it up in these two principles:

- "Goods, even when legitimately owned, always have a universal destination; any type of improper accumulation is immoral, because it openly contradicts the universal destination assigned to all goods by the Creator."
- "Riches fulfill their function of service to man when they are destined to produce benefits for others and for society."

UNFAIR DISMISSAL

Catholic social doctrine is often unfairly dismissed as socialism or worse, and as hostile to a free enterprise market economy. The tradition respects human freedom and individual initiative, however; it recognizes the efficiencies of markets and the role they can play in curbing individual excess. But the tradition is both realistic and compassionate in denouncing rigid capitalism and abuses of power. It supports both order and freedom in economic activity while insisting on justice, particularly for the poor. It favors no one economic system over any other. It recognizes that any system is populated by people and therefore this tradition of Catholic social doctrine speaks to the hearts and minds of human persons who make, for better or worse, economic decisions that have an impact on the lives of others.

So this brings us back to wealth and responsibility. The wealth is really the Lord's; the responsibility is clearly ours. Understanding justice principles, as explained in the last chapter, is an important first stage of reflection for those who possess wealth. Subsequent stages of reflection can carry the haves responsibly, step by step, through a complex world of personal and national economic decision making. We will be measured personally and nationally by the uprightness (justice) of those decisions.

With this as an interpretive framework, it is up to us, who accept it, to begin applying it. It can function as a range-finder in setting personal goals for pursuit of the good life. It can serve as a prompter for decisions about production, consumption, savings, and investment. It can provide an outlook for the shaping of legislation and regulation, as well as a norm for vocational, political, and philanthropic choice.

It will certainly affect our assimilation of (and—on any give day—our reaction to) news reports of what is happening in our world.

14

■

The Good Life

Mention of the *good life* in the next to last paragraph of the previous chapter, takes me back in memory to Graduation Day at the University of Portland, May 2, 2004. It was my privilege to deliver the commencement address on that occasion. I invited the graduates to test their personal understanding of what constituted the good life. Here are my words to them.

....

In the interest of full disclosure, as I stand here in the midst of *summa*, *magna*, and *cum laude* graduating seniors, and as I find myself surrounded by gold and silver academic medalists here at the University of Portland, I must admit that when I was in college many years ago, I occupied a place in the all-important bottom half of the class that made the top half possible. So let's hear it for that indispensable bottom half of this class as we salute all of you graduating seniors!

I recognize that a commencement address is a fifteen-minute interruption delaying the progress of a battalion of happy young people on their forward march to a great party. So I shall speak with one admiring eye on you, and the other on the clock that allots to me a privileged measure of your time on this great day.

Using the full authority you have vested in me by virtue of your invitation to speak on this happy occasion, I declare each one of you to be the world's leading expert on your own opinion. And I ask each of you now to formulate an opinion, a personal opinion capable of becoming a personal conviction, in response to this Commencement Day question: How do you understand the good life? What, in your opinion, are the elements that constitute the good life?

The question might prompt you to think about the Golden Rule.

Those of you who have examined other cultures and other faiths might have discovered, in the Analects of Confucius, the question I just raised expressed this way: "Is there any one word that can serve as a principle for the conduct of life?" To which Confucius replied: "Reciprocity. Do not do to others what you would not want others to do to you."

You may have come across this saying of Rabbi Hillel: "What is hateful to you do not do to your neighbor; that is the whole Torah, while the rest is commentary thereof."

Atticus Finch, early in the novel *To Kill a Mockingbird*, gave his young daughter Scout some advice—that any of your parents might have given you—when he said: "If you can learn a simple trick, Scout, you'll get along a lot better with all kinds of folks. You never really understand a person until you consider things from his point of view... until you climb into his skin and walk around in it." There you have another clue to assist you in your discovery of what constitutes the good life—sensitivity, empathy, and concern for others.

LOVE ONE ANOTHER

No need to remind you here, in a Catholic college, that the founder of Christianity told his followers that his commandment was this: "Love one another as I have loved you." And in another place he said you can find your life only if you're willing to lose it in service to others.

You've had the opportunity to reflect and grow here in your student days at the University of Portland. Friendships have deepened over the years. So, too, have convictions. That's why it is timely today to examine your convictions about the good life. If you are convinced that the easy life is the good and happy life, you missed something that the University of Portland has been telling you. If you spell out your formula for the good life in terms of money, pleasure, and power, you have written for yourself a formula for frustration; you have painted yourself into a horizonless corner; you have stepped into a box that will seal you off from the joy of living.

The good life, the really good life, is a life lived generously in the service of others. I suspect your young hearts might be telling you that today. And I suspect you are wise enough to fear the "mind-forged manacles" of materialism that could trap the unsuspecting. No one is totally immune to the virus of materialism, but your University of Portland education has given you adequate protection against that affliction. UP has encouraged you to cultivate a life of the mind, a lively faith, and a generous spirit. You yearn to live a life of love understood not in a dreamy romantic way, but in a practical, daily, down-to-earth way of keeping your commitments and your promises and being of generous service to others.

There is a lot that is special about the University of Portland. One element in your campus culture and tradition that is central is the presence of the Madonna. No, not *that* Madonna (the one delivered on request by Google or Yahoo search engines). You know the one I have in mind. Deep in the University of Portland tradition, the Madonna, Mary the mother of Jesus, the Jewish maiden, is present. She is, and has been since 1901, the patroness of your University. She has been patroness of the Congregation of Holy Cross, your sponsoring religious community, since its beginning in 1837. She is depicted in mosaic art on campus in Christ the Teacher chapel, in iconography in the chapel in Corrado Hall, in sculpture in the Marian Garden next to your campus chapel. Your Madonna is Mary. She goes with you when you leave campus today.

As you go, reflect for a moment on the fact that Mary's love was there in both her smile and her tears. You see it in Madonna-and-Child art; you see it in Michelangelo's Pietà. There is a famous Burrell collection of art in Glasgow, Scotland. A poet, Peter Granger-Banyard, visited that museum often and caught the spirit of your Madonna in these words in a poem titled, "At the Burrell Collection":

> Beside a pillar stands
> A pale French limestone Madonna:
> Tall and crowned
> She proudly holds her lively child:
> Her love is in her smile.
> Beyond, against the wall,
> A German painted limewood Pietà:
> Racked and bowed
> Mary cradles the corpse that is still her son:
> Her love is in her tears.

That's you. That's life—*the good life*—love in your smile; love in your tears. You are ready for that. You are no longer youngsters, you smiling and perhaps momentarily tearful graduates; you are, as you so well know, young adults, well prepared to meet life in the real world of smiles and tears.

FREE TO CHOOSE

Your young adulthood is, in truth, a special trust. Think a bit about what it really means to be an adult. You're free now of childhood fears. You should be free of impulsive activity. Prejudice should, by now, have relaxed its grip on you. You are autonomous, not totally independent, just autonomous—a freestanding adult capable of relating disinterestedly to others, of putting others' interests ahead of your own, of serving others. You are free to choose; that means freedom to choose wisely or not well. You can choose self-service and self-enclosure, or you can choose to have regard for others, to be compassionate toward others, to live for others.

Only an adult can begin to understand the meaning of sacrifice. And only sacrifice can unlock the deepest meaning of love. Like the Madonna, there will be love in your smiles, love in your tears, and love—in the form of sacrifice—in your understanding of the good life.

Jesus taught that there is no greater love than the love that involves a willingness to lay down one's life for one's friend. We tend to think of that in terms of heroic, once-and-for-all self-sacrifice. Not so. There are countless adults who lay down their lives for others day by day—for spouses, for children, for students like you, for elderly parents, for workplace associates, for helpless and needy human beings. Your graduation certifies you as capable of meeting the demands of smiling self-donation. The wisdom you acquired here at the University of Portland will convince you that your happiness depends on your willingness to sacrifice.

So spell out for yourself, in a quiet moment today or tomorrow, your understanding of the good life. Make sure that it is a conviction, not just a concept. And if that conviction says that love for you is sacrifice, and sacrifice is love, then I declare you not just to be the world's leading expert on your own opinion; I declare you to be ready for a productive and happy life in the post-commencement world. Congratulations!

....

That Commencement Day question—"What is your idea of the good life, the really good life?"—is worth considering by all Americans in every stage of life, indeed by human persons everywhere. The quality of our answers, worldwide, will be a good indicator of how long we're going to have to wait for justice and peace to make their home among us.

15

Workplace Spirituality

It seems fairly obvious to me that all Christians are expected to bring their Sunday faith into their Monday-through-Friday workplaces. But, in order to do that, most have to make themselves more aware—more attentive to the fact that their daily work can positively influence their religious faith. Thinking about Sunday-into-Monday is one thing; taking a Monday-up-to-Sunday approach to the question of workplace spirituality is something else again. It is no small challenge. Ignatius of Loyola laid out that challenge centuries ago in the form of a spirituality based on the grace to "find God in all things."

God is there to be found in the world of work. The daily finding of God in the things of work can deepen one's faith and quite literally ground it in the familiar reality that becomes an altar from which an offering of praise and thanks is made.

It seems to me that working Americans who enjoy relative security and affluence, are all too easily distracted from God during the week and not all that convinced that they have anything to declare before God on weekends. Successful and relatively secure in their jobs, many of our contemporaries are insufficiently aware of their need for God. Many of them are like the affluent farm family in Jane Smiley's (1992) *A Thousand Acres.* (If you own a farm that size—one thousand acres—you have made it, you are part of the farm establishment.) In the novel, the narrator-daughter of a farmer-father who successfully took unpromising land and with the benefit of hard work, innovation, and application of expensive technology, made it a successful farming operation, explains that on Sundays, "We went to church to pay our respects, not to give thanks."

A reflective, sensitive, gratitude-driven journey of faith beginning anew every Monday will bring the believer to Sunday in a state of mind far different from that of the family that went to church just to pay its respects. Without an abiding sense of our dependence upon God for all we are and do, without an ever deeper sense of gratitude toward God, we run the risk of falling into the pattern of dropping in on Sundays to pay our respects, instead of coming before the altar to give faith-filled thanks based on an abiding awareness that everything we have—*everything*—has come to us from God. This is a lesson that can be taught and learned only in the language of the faithful heart, the language of spirituality.

In Alice McDermott's (1998, 92–94) prize-winning novel *Charming Billy*, you'll read the following views about the world of work attributed by the narrator to Mrs. Holtzman, the mother of Billy's cousin Dennis: "She objected to the monotony of nine-to-five, the tedium, the hours and days you ended up wishing away, swinging from one Saturday morning to another like a monkey at the zoo. In part, it was the anonymity: ... once you boarded the subway or the bus or joined the crawling stream of automobiles or found your space in the revolving door, the elevator, behind the desk or the counter or the machine, you became what you really were—you became, when you got right down to it, what you really were: one of the so many million, just one more...[on] a slow march to an unremarkable end."

This line of thinking is not based on anything resembling a functioning workplace spirituality. No one of us is "just one more" anywhere, at any time, including all the time we spend at work. Each one of us is a unique creation. We are unique human beings, not human doings, but we are called to do something special. We are called to be and do in the world of work—enriching, extending, enlarging, by Gods grace, the wherewithal God has given us, that which we know as our world of work.

THE PAULINE CRITERIA

In his letter to the Galatians, Paul addresses people who are converts from paganism. He instructs them in the exercise of their newly found freedom in the Holy Spirit and urges them to "live by the Spirit" in their normal secular surroundings. This is precisely what serious Christians at work in the world today are concerned about doing.

How can a person know that he or she is guided by the Spirit in the world of work? Paul offers in Galatians 5:22–23 what I think of as the Pauline criteria for judging the consistency of one's own (or anyone else's) behavior with the presence of the Spirit in a human life. They constitute what Paul calls the fruit of the Spirit. There are nine of them and Paul lists them in this order: love, joy, peace, patience, kindness, generosity, faithfulness, gentleness, and self-control.

Examine what happens in the workplace against these criteria. These are non-market values that can humanize every marketplace and workplace. All nine of these Pauline characteristics are within the reach of normal people leading ordinary lives.

In contrast to these ingredients of a faith-based spirituality rooted in Christian revelation, Paul mentions the works of the flesh, i.e., human activity only—activity not informed by God's indwelling Spirit. The works of the flesh are what we are left with when we reject the Spirit and set out blindly on our own. These rebel elements are obvious, Paul notes, and he identifies them as follows: "immorality, impurity, licentiousness, idolatry, sorcery, hatreds, rivalry, jealousy, outbursts of fury, acts of selfishness, dissensions, factions, occasions of envy, drinking bouts, orgies, and the like." At the end of this catalogue, Paul puts it bluntly: "I warn you, as I warned you before, that those who do such things will not inherit the kingdom of God" (Gal. 5:19–21).

After examining Paul's second list, some might be forgiven for thinking, "Well, orgies aside, that's actually a pretty fair description of the workplace as I know it!" It really isn't, of course, but the description is sometimes close enough to the mark to motivate reflective persons to give the first list of positive Pauline values a closer look.

If Christian spirituality is to mean anything at all in the workplace, the Pauline criteria signaling the presence of the Spirit should be the very infrastructure the Christian carries into the world of work. They should be guiding principles, pillars that support a working life. Once internalized, they can serve as answers from within—from mind, soul, and spirit—to challenges to faith raised by circumstances in the world of work.

The Pauline criteria can both protect and transform a person, who, thus transformed, can transform the workplace. Interaction with other persons as well as with materials and difficulties in the workplace, can help shape these transforming principles within a faith-committed worker.

Sober reflection on the absence in either workplace or worker of these positive criteria can be unsettling. So can the realization of the occasional presence of what Paul listed as negatives. These experiences *should* be unsettling. Welcome the discomfort. It can serve an eviction notice on the complacency that can stifle both the Spirit and the spirituality waiting to energize the man or woman of faith.

A PRACTICE-ORIENTED SPIRITUALITY

Robert Wuthnow (1998, 3–4,168–70), a sociologist of religion, sees spirituality to be moving in a new direction. His book, *After Heaven: Spirituality in America Since the 1950s*, describes a shift from a spirituality of *dwelling* with an emphasis on *habitation* to a spirituality of *seeking* with an emphasis on *negotiation*. The dwellers relate to sacred space; the seekers "search for sacred moments that reinforce their conviction that the divine exists, but these moments are fleeting; rather than knowing the territory, people explore new spiritual vistas, and they may have to negotiate among complex and confusing meanings of spirituality." For the seekers, "rather than being in a place that is by definition spiritual, the sacred is found momentarily in experiences as different as mowing the lawn or viewing a full moon."

In his final chapter, Wuthnow proposes an alternative to the dwelling-oriented and the seeking-oriented spiritualities, and that alternative is what he calls a *practice-oriented* spirituality. Dwelling-oriented spirituality is not doing it today for many Americans who are beset with "a sense of spiritual homelessness." But the seeking-oriented spirituality is not satisfactory either because it "results in a transient spiritual existence characterized more often by dabbling than by depth."

"To say that spirituality is practiced means that people engage intentionally in activities that deepen their relationship to the sacred." Wuthnow explains further:

> Broadly conceived, spiritual practice is a cluster of intentional activities concerned with relating to the sacred. Although it may result in extraordinary or miraculous experiences, it generally takes place in ordinary life. In the sixteenth century Ignatius Loyola described it as a "method of examination of conscience, of meditation, of contemplation, of vocal and mental prayers, and [a] way of preparing and disposing the soul to rid itself of all inordinate attachments, and, after their removal, of seeking and finding the will of God." How these activities are performed and understood has varied enormously in different cultural and religious traditions.... A focus on practice helps orient our thinking to the fact that spirituality also exists in the complex and fragmented arena of contemporary society. Commuting, dual careers, and busy family schedules have added complexity to many people's lives..., but spiritual practice remains possible in the midst of these challenging circumstances.

Practices are obviously more portable than are sacred places, but a practice-oriented spirituality is not necessarily a total break from a dwelling-place orientation. To some extent, believers can take their sacred space with them. Practice-oriented spirituality also differs from the seeker variety by providing a more orderly and sustainable approach to the sacred.

For contemporary Christians in the workplace, the forward march, Monday on through the week into Sunday, will have reference points in the dwelling places of past religious experience, as well as in the journey metaphor congenial to the pilgrimage of faith. Some sort of handbook of method and practice, emerging from one's own experience, will surely help maintain progress in the offertory procession that is continuously moving through the world of work toward the altar of God.

16

Spirituality and the Social Question

Bill Droel, leader of the Chicago-based National Center for the Laity, said to me about a decade ago that "what Pope John Paul II called the Gospel of Work is not a salient feature of the spirituality of most Catholics—at least that is the observation of the National Center for the Laity." He mentioned this while inviting me to participate in a workshop designed to explore the theme "Monday into Sunday," a direction on the faith journey that I touched upon in the last chapter and that Droel prefers to the more familiar one-day spillover of Sunday into Monday. He is interested in a work-to-faith movement, not the more familiar reflective route that traces the relevance of religious faith to the world of work.

I was there for the Chicago workshop and found participants prepared to put themselves into a pondering process that envisioned something of an offertory procession that starts on Monday and moves through the full workweek up to a Sunday opportunity to place one's gift, enhanced by a week of work, at the altar.

Bill Droel asked me what I thought it would take "to integrate the Church's social mission into the daily habits (mind, spirit, and behavior)" of Catholics in the workplace. I gave that question a lot of thought as I recalled that very early in his pontificate, John Paul II (1981) told the world that human work is "a key, probably the essential key, to the whole social question" (No. 3).

All Christians are expected to bring their Sunday faith to their Monday work. But most, as I indicated in the last chapter, have to make themselves more attentive to the fact that their daily work can positively influence their religious faith.

THE GOSPEL OF WORK

Gospel of Work is an expression that organizers of the National Center for the Laity's workshop prefer to *spirituality of work*. There is nothing wrong, of course, with the expression *workplace spirituality*; workshop planners were simply concerned that participants beware of letting their ponderings take an individualistic route, and that they not permit the pursuit of the quiet virtues to distract them from the demands of justice in the world of work.

Where is the Gospel of Work to be found? In the workplace—the same place where you find God. You can also find it expressed in sacred Scripture when read with care. Take for example, the fourth Gospel's twenty-first chapter, the account of the post-resurrection meeting of the apostles and Jesus at the lakeside. At the opening of this incident, you find the apostles restless and a bit uneasy. Jesus had already appeared to them in the Upper Room. They knew he had risen from the dead. They also knew that he would somehow or other show up from time to time, but they didn't know when. Simon Peter said to the others, "I'm going fishing." It was not recreational fishing he had in mind. He said to them, in effect, that he, professional fisherman that he was, was going back to work. And, of course, it was while he was at work that he encountered the Lord.

If Christian spirituality is to mean anything at all in the workplace, the Pauline criteria—that signal the presence of the Spirit, and that I listed in the last chapter—should be the very infrastructure the Christian carries into the world of work. These virtues should be guiding principles—pillars that support a working life. Once internalized, they can serve as answers from within—from mind, soul, and spirit—to challenges to faith raised by circumstances in the world of work.

The Pauline criteria can both protect and transform a person, who, thus transformed, can transform the workplace. Interaction with other persons as well as with materials and difficulties in the workplace can help shape these transforming principles within a faith-committed worker.

ASKING THE SOCIAL QUESTION

We all need clarity on the true meaning of Paul's nine positive but quiet virtues: love, joy, peace, patience, kindness, generosity, faithfulness, gentleness, and self-control. We also need to take time to think about the noisier virtues like justice and fortitude, if we are to integrate, as the Chicago workshop participants were invited to do, the Church's social mission into our daily habits—mind, spirit, and behavior. We need to connect the Church's social *credenda* with the Church's social *agenda*. And a helpful step in that direction is to start thinking about that time-honored expression in Catholic social thought, the *social question*.

What is the social question in our day? In a sense, we asked it in our chapter fourteen inquiry about the good life. That is one way of raising the social question. For Pope Leo XIII in 1891, the social question focused on the condition of the working classes, on the right of workers to form associations, to organize themselves into unions and other protective arrangements against assaults on their human dignity from the new industrialization and the threat of socialism. In 1967 Pope Paul VI said in *Populorum Progressio*, "Today the principal fact that we must all recognize is that the social question has become worldwide" (No. 3). But what precisely was then, and is now, the question?

At the most general level, I think the social question should be stated this way. *How can the human community of persons and nations live together in peace secured by justice?* The protection of fundamental human dignity requires that the question be asked at all times. The organization of human life requires that it be asked in all areas of human activity.

Anyone concerned about integrating the Church's social mission into daily life—into habits of mind, outlook, and behavior—has to give serious thought to what form the social question might be taking today in the workplace.

In family life, the social question, as I see it, is how to shore up the interpersonal commitments that make marriages permanent and thus create an environment of stability for spouses and children. But what about commitment and cooperation in the world of work?

Take your pick of the most urgent or pressing social question today in the economic arena. Our Church puts the poor in a preferential position; we talk about an option for the poor—preferential protection for the poor. As economic life grows more complex, the danger of damage to human fulfillment and dignity rises accordingly. Both the economic organization and the task it exacts can stifle human initiative. This is the stuff of a good social question. Another formulation of the social question in the economic sphere would ask how we might contain the virus of materialism in the world community and in all of its separate political and familial parts.

In *Pacem in Terris*, Pope John XXIII remarked that women "will not tolerate being treated as mere material instruments, but demand rights befitting a human person in domestic and public life" (No. 71). The contemporary workplace poses threats to reduce both men and women to "mere material instruments." But with an eye to women at work today, we might ask, in our effort to articulate the social question: What is the meaning of woman in any society? Why is the value of woman an issue in contemporary society? Why is it a struggle today for women to assert their rights and assume duties worthy of their full human personhood?

MOVING OUTWARD

Everyone in the Catholic faith community should have something to say about the social question—raising the right questions and forming workable answers. We should, of course, get to work on the personal task of making sure our personal values are right, that we keep the commitments we make, that we respect life in all its forms, and that the territory between our ears and beneath our feet can, so far as it is in our power to choose, be marked by the reign of justice and peace.

But that is not enough. We have to move outward. We have to avoid the trap of withdrawal from the fray. Every significant social question can be traced to fault lines in human institutions. Only by working within those institutions can the fault lines be repaired. Only by participation in human processes (political, for the most part) can we create new institutions to provide just exchanges, promote just relationships, and provide peace.

17

Religion and Politics

More and more Catholic conversations through the summer and into the fall of 2004 centered on religion and politics. That was natural enough in an election year, but I wondered then and continue to ask how Catholics would answer the question posed in a newspaper headline I saw in that election season: "Does God Belong in Politics?" "Yes, of course," I found myself saying. "Politics is people and God is in all people, so surely God belongs in politics." Without the people, how can God's will work in our world? If God is present in every person, how can God not be in politics?

We all pray each day, "Thy kingdom come." We know that it is a kingdom of love, justice, and peace that's been promised to us. We also know that the kingdom is the reign of God, and that God reigns when our wills—individually and collectively—are in proper alignment with his. That's why reasoned, well-constructed moral arguments are so important in the formation of public policy. Threat, force, and ridicule won't do it; moral reasoning will.

When Jesus stepped into his public life (Mark 1:14) he announced: "The Kingdom of God is at hand." He added, "Repent, therefore, and believe the Gospel." I often think that it is tragic that a kingdom of love, justice, and peace has been at hand these many centuries but not yet grasped. And I can only conclude that the delay in the coming of the promised kingdom is our refusal to repent, to accept a value reversal, an attitudinal turnaround in response to Gospel values. This would convince us to lower the barriers within ourselves—namely, the opposites of love, justice, and peace that we harbor within—and thus open ourselves, individually and as a nation, to the promised kingdom that will indeed come, but only in God's own time and God's own way. Politics is part of the process that should be moving us in the right direction, but I'm not at all encouraged by the quality of reasoning I find in most political debates.

Although there is a separation of church and state that is quite appropriate in the United States, there is, as I mentioned earlier in this book, no separation between church and society. The Church, in my view, should be doing a better job in communicating Gospel values to society and then trusting society to make political decisions that are consistent with those values.

I think it is inaccurate to speak of *building* the kingdom. We can, as the popular hymn puts it, "build the City of God," but not the kingdom. All we can do is lower the barriers within ourselves to the coming of the promised kingdom; we cannot build what only God can give.

THE POLITICAL AGENDA

There is work to be done now in building the City of God and the political agenda is not unrelated to that work. Issues on the political agenda are multiple and diverse. No one issue alone will pave a sure and smooth road for the coming of the promised Kingdom.

Speaking from the side of religion to the issues that were debated in the 2004 presidential campaign (or any campaign, for that matter), I would hold up the Beatitudes (Matt. 5:1–12) as a checklist. You can review the Beatitudes back in chapter two—they deal with the poor in spirit, peacemakers, the meek, the quest for justice, etc. How does a given candidate or political party fare in the comparison of their programs or policy proposals with the Beatitude values? Few serious, faith-committed voters, who are doing their best to assimilate Gospel values and bring them to life in this imperfect world, will say they've found a perfect fit.

The Church should stay out of partisan politics but not hesitate for a moment to suggest that Beatitude values belong in a good society, and that Beatitude principles can inform the moral reasoning needed to shape solid public policies.

Catholic bishops and Catholic politicians had some tensions in the 2004 presidential election year. Those tensions remain. There continues to be talk about voting records and related worthiness or unworthiness to approach the communion table. Several bishops want to deny a place at the table of the Lord to Catholic citizens who vote for candidates whose positions on some public policy issues can be taken as moral stances contrary to the teachings of the Catholic Church.

My reaction to these controversies brings to mind the funeral of a Catholic friend about fifteen years ago. She was only fifty, a victim of cancer. The church in northern Virginia was packed with friends; most, but not all, were Catholics. At Communion time, the pastor, who in black cassock and lace surplice was observing but not concelebrating, stepped up to the microphone at the lectern and announced: "Only Roman Catholics in the state of grace may come forward at this time to receive Holy Communion."

Afterwards, a prominent Washington, D.C. television news anchorman, who was a close friend of the deceased, remarked to me, "I thought he had some kind of an ecclesiastical metal detector all set up to buzz away the unworthies!"

(No progress to date, so far as I know, on the design and manufacture of such a device.)

Another memory that comes to mind, as points of view on the communion controversy were exchanged, is a story I once heard about visits paid to former House Speaker Tip O'Neill by several bishops in connection with the annual Right-to-Life March in Washington. They wanted Tip O'Neill, a devout Catholic (who, as Speaker, rarely voted) to be aware of the evil of abortion and do what he could to ban it. "Now that's a serious moral issue you're talking about, isn't it," the Speaker would ask. "You bet it is," they responded. "Well, isn't that your job—to educate the people about the evil of abortion? If you succeed in your moral instruction and persuasion, abortion won't be the political issue it is."

NO THREATS, NO RIDICULE

O'Neill had a point. And, of course, so did the bishops in bringing their concern to their elected representative. Catholic bishops and Catholic politicians should be talking to each other in a no-threat, low-temperature, constructive conversation. As I noted more than once earlier in this book, the Jesuit theologian John Courtney Murray was fond of quoting the Dominican philosopher Thomas Gilby's remark that "civilizations rest on citizens locked in moral argument." Faith-informed, well-reasoned moral arguments for public policy positions are what Catholic leaders, ecclesiastical and political, should be exchanging, not threats and ridicule.

Meanwhile, I think *participation* should be the word from Catholic leaders to their followers in any political season. Participation rates in elections at all levels in America are disturbingly low. Catholic teaching says there is a moral obligation on the part of citizens to participate in the policy-formation processes in a representative democracy. Catholics should be reminded by their bishops of their moral obligation to participate, i.e., at the least, to register and to vote. Catholics should continue to look to their Church, their schools, families, and personal experience in moral decision-making for help in the formation of their own consciences. They should not be instructed for whom or how to vote; they need only be encouraged to vote in accordance with their well-formed consciences.

The moral education Tip O'Neill urged the bishops to provide will be helpful in shaping the political judgments that only the individual voter can make. In our representative democracy the individual, as citizen and/or elected official, has to make that judgment for him- or herself.

Without conscientious participation, the truth will never have the votes to prevail.

18

Becoming Ever More Human

The Council of Independent Colleges confers annually an Academic Leadership Award at a national conference for chief academic officers of independent colleges. I was the recipient of this award at Williamsburg, Virginia on November 6, 1999. Their questionable judgment in honoring me gave me a great opportunity to speak to higher education administrators who oversee and promote quality in the undergraduate curriculum. I spoke to them about the process of becoming ever more human in the wonderful world of higher education.

I reminded this audience that it was John Gardner, former Secretary of Health, Education, and Welfare (as our present Department of Health and Human Services was once known) and founder of Common Cause, who remarked, decades earlier in a commencement address at Cornell, that historians would look back to the troubled decade of the sixties and note that higher education in the United States was caught in those years in a "savage crossfire between unloving critics and uncritical lovers." The unloving critics, Gardner explained, wanted to destroy the institutions with no thought of what would replace them; the uncritical lovers wanted to protect the institutions from any change at all, even though the protective embrace would, in fact, smother them. Higher education seems to have survived that critical period in reasonably good shape. Future success, however, depended, I said, on the ability of educators to encourage the cultivation of character during the collegiate years through the development of intellect.

I did not mean to suggest that character was not being developed nor that there was an absence of rigor in the intellectual programs under the supervision of these educational leaders. My point was simply to say that you don't have to be ill to get better. There is always room for improvement. No true academic wants to leave to the student-life professionals—colleagues on the other side of the academic street, so to speak—full responsibility for attending to a broad and familiar spectrum of campus behavioral issues ranging from civility to sobriety. The academic side has something important to contribute in this regard by providing challenging intellectual programs, by offering, on the part of professors, good personal example of integrity and intellectual curiosity, and high academic expectations for all students. Professors and their colleagues in student life should, I said, be working on this issue of character development together.

If the *New York Times* (March 3, 1999) is to be believed, "Three decades after American college students defiantly threw off the vestiges of curfews, dress codes, and dormitory house mothers, a revolution is under way in undergraduate life that may be quieter but no less significant." Under a headline that reads, "In a Revolution of New Rules for Students, Colleges Are Turning Full Circle," the report states, "What is evolving is a tamer campus and an updated and subtler version of *in loco parentis*—the concept that educators are stand-in parents. College administrators are struggling with the two questions that are emerging as central: Are undergraduates really adults? And should they be seen as the college's customers or more as its product?"

As the parent of any adolescent knows, it is difficult to say exactly where trust ends and neglect begins; so to avoid neglect, parents typically tend to yield on trust and tighten up on control. I encouraged these educators, regardless of whether they accepted an *in loco parentis* role, and regardless of whether or not students expect such a role of them, never to give up on trusting the young. Just rest your trust on a principled approach to your responsibilities, I said, a principled approach that respects the dignity of every student and sees each student as occupying his or her own unique stage of human development. They will disappoint us occasionally, but don't sell them short. Students are not yet full adults, they have to be viewed as works in progress. It is a mistake to regard them as purchasers of academic services entitled to full consumer satisfaction on their own terms. High standards can be set in mutually agreed-upon terms of trade.

I had just finished reading a book by David Fromkin (1999), professor of international relations, history, and law at Boston University. This ambitious book bears the title *The Way of the World: From the Dawn of Civilizations to the Eve of the Twenty-first Century*. The book's subtitle is a measure of its author's ambition, but his skills enabled him to cover and synthesize, with clarity and style, millions of years in the relatively short span of 222 pages—a book short in length, but not on insight.

The book was well received by the *New York Times* (January 17, 1999), whose reviewer, William R. Everdell, stimulated— with the following summary—my desire to read it:

> Fromkin distinguishes eight stages in universal history, most of them hinging on events historians of many stripes can agree on as the most significant in the history of humankind: the emergence of the hominid line, apes with brains, in prehistoric Africa ("Becoming Human"); the discovery of agriculture and the creation of the first cities—settlements whose residents were not all farmers ("Inventing Civilization"); the sudden rise of universalizing religious and moral systems all over civilized Eurasia in the sixth century B.C. ("Developing a Conscience"); the birth of the idea of world civilization with the empires of ancient Eurasia ("Seeking a Lasting Peace"); the rise of rationalism and empirical science ("Achieving Rationality"); the irreversible encounter, after the fifteenth century, between human societies in Eurasia and Africa and those in the Americas ("Uniting the Planet"); the industrial modernization that began in the eighteenth century ("Releasing Nature's Energies"); and finally the steady movement toward democratic government centered in the nineteenth century and the unsteady movement toward decolonization and world law in the twentieth ("Ruling Ourselves").

The first four of those chapter headings look to the past: "Becoming Human," "Inventing Civilization," "Developing a Conscience," and "Seeking a Lasting Peace." The next four look to the present: "Achieving Rationality," "Uniting the Planet," "Releasing Nature's Energies," and "Ruling Ourselves." All eight of those headings strike me as useful pegs upon which to hang some reflections on the condition of student academic life in contemporary American higher education. They can be considered as eight windows through which one can observe student academic life. I recognize, of course, that genuine education takes place on both sides of the campus street; I simply chose to focus on the side that is dominated by classroom buildings, libraries, and laboratories.

Consider the relevance, to that side of campus life, of all that is involved in becoming human, inventing civilization, developing a conscience, seeking peace, achieving rationality, uniting the planet, releasing nature's energies, and ruling ourselves. They have supreme relevance to the strictly academic side of the house.

BECOMING HUMAN

It is helpful to recall that when the incoming freshmen begin college they are only four years out of the eighth grade! They can be managed and taught. Most really want to be there. Just about all are well-prepared and ready, but not one of them is yet fully an adult.

When they arrive on campus, first-time college students are, of course, already human beings, despite some early evidence to the contrary in August and September of freshman year. They are, however, still *becoming* human. They are on campus precisely because they (or their parents) decided that they do indeed have human potential that is ripe for further development. That development will take place on the intellectual front under the guidance and encouragement of professors; there will also be development on the social, interpersonal, spiritual, and psychological fronts under the guidance of student-life professionals, who are colleagues with the faculty in the formation and education enterprise.

What is the environment that should be provided to facilitate this growth? Class schedules and class size can shape or impede that growth. Yet, some academic vice presidents and deans, with the complicity of department chairs, may arrange these things more for the convenience of faculty than the best academic interest of students. Those who are deeply concerned about these matters may have to fight facilities administrators, budget officers, and top management for the time and space needed to allow the students to grow. Aesthetics, too, are important. So is population density in classrooms, labs, and libraries. The academy's architecture, on both sides of the campus street, can be a friend or foe of student academic development.

Most campuses need more of whatever it is in a building that fosters the becoming-human side of students

They are not apes; they are in the process of becoming fully human. They can and will respond to creative persuasion and encouragement to attend to their longer-term interests.

INVENTING CIVILIZATION

The discovery of agriculture and the establishment of town-like settlements where not all residents were farmers was a consequence of the end of the Ice Age ten or fifteen thousand years ago. Hunting and gathering gave way to farming and more permanent dwellings. Wheels, carts, and plows enhanced productivity. Not everyone was needed to produce the food; some were freed for arts, and crafts, and trade.

Although some few of today's college students think food is grown in the basements of supermarkets, all are sufficiently familiar with ancient history to know that the discovery of agriculture led the way to the creation of the first cities. They also acknowledge that some others produce and prepare their food, and they recognize dependency upon (if not gratitude toward) others—for providing the basics necessary for undistracted life in pursuit of academic goals. They pursue those goals in campus communities, some much like towns or small cities.

The Greek word for city, *polis*, provides an etymological clue to subsequent developments that relate to words like *polite* (behavior expected of those now clustered into closer quarters); *policy* (guidelines necessary for orderly group activity); *police* (those who enforce the rules); *politicians* (those who devote most of their energies to policy formation, legislation, and pursuit of group objectives).

Professors and deans are, so to speak, the civil servants responsible for the smooth functioning of the academic side of the campus polis. It is their vision, example, and encouragement that cultivate *polite* academic behavior. It is their wisdom that produces and applies intelligent *policies* to guide academic development. They *police* student achievement with grading systems, honor systems, and the various rewards and punishments designed to encourage intellectual growth. They are, year after year, from their privileged positions of influence, *inventing civilization*.

DEVELOPING A CONSCIENCE

With the rise of civilization came religion and philosophy, and with them came the development and articulation of moral conscience. Classroom lectures, great books, and moral arguments in appropriate academic forums can engage college students in the formation of conscience, in the discovery of right and wrong in human behavior—as displayed in history, in literature, and in themselves. On the other side of the campus street, they will have abundant opportunity to practice their moral principles or, in some sad cases, to discover their deficits in this regard. Relativism is no solution. As it is often said, if you stand for nothing, you'll fall for anything. The academic program helps the young discover that which is really worth standing for.

Campus cultures are defined by dominant values. Those values can be materialistic; they can focus on greed, power, and the lust for pleasure, possessions, and prestige. They can be respectful or disdainful of human dignity. Faculty, as facilitators of growth in all that it takes to become fully human, have to be concerned that they are not overseeing a value-vacant curriculum.

Will there be differences of conviction as to what is right and wrong in specific circumstances? Of course, there will be. The point to establish, however, is that moral arguments, not prejudice or passion, are expected to underlie those personally held positions. Personal integrity requires that one live his or her life truthfully, true to the deepest values and convictions that are freely held by the responsible person who is in the process of becoming ever more human through the process of human moral choice. That process should be taking place in the curricular programs that faculty provide.

SEEKING A LASTING PEACE

In world history, empires emerged and those in one empire had to learn to live in peace with others. In addition to kingdoms or empires, there were city-states and republics, all far removed from ancient tribes. All these had their leaders; they also had their external friends and foes. At this point in the advance of civilization, say a half century or so before the Christian era, it became noticeable that loyalty kept things together within, and hostility (not just suspicion) focused on the outsiders.

Campuses have their empires, as we all know; they also have their versions of city-states and republics with shifting leadership but fairly constant loyalties. Factions can emerge and fights can erupt almost anywhere at any time on college and university campuses. When these are unavoidable, civility has to rule, and that won't happen without faculty cooperation and participation. Wherever human nature is present, there is a potential for difference and even dispute. This is no reason for despair; it is only out of difference that union can be achieved.

ACHIEVING RATIONALITY

When the minds of men and women—sometimes in pairs, often in groups—are engaged with one another (locked, if you will, in reasoned argument), civility reigns and civilized society prospers. Rationality is indeed an achievement. Responsibility for cultivating the development of a rational mind during the collegiate experience rests primarily with faculty. The cultivation happens formally and regularly in classrooms and libraries.

One way of measuring the challenge faculty face, in fostering the life of the mind in classroom settings, is to consider the out-of-class, out-of-library hours their students spend on campus.

Estimate, for instance, the monetary value of the audio-video electronic equipment they have in their rooms (along with tapes, discs, i-pods, cell phones, and all sorts of entertainment software) over against the monetary value of printed matter on their dorm-room shelves. The ratio might be about two hundred to one; it is anyone's guess. Well, you might say, that is hardly surprising; they have well-stocked libraries and resource centers on campus, and they are in the dorms to relax and rest. True enough. But what about the art of conversation? What about discussion and debate—reasoned argument on important issues? What about opportunities for the developing youngster to talk to others about his or her childhood, family customs, religious traditions, moral convictions?

Creative programming is needed in dormitories and student unions. Faculty cooperation with student-life professionals in developing that programming should be encouraged.

The President of Penn State University set a great example for all academic leaders some years ago when, as I understand it, he simply decided to have bundles of good newspapers delivered to residence halls each morning for free distribution to students. Give them something good to read and just trust that the newspaper habit will eventually form. Without creating a budgetary burden, this creative gesture serves to encourage both the life of the mind and the art of conversation. It helps, in other words, to move closer to the goal of achieving rationality.

UNITING THE PLANET

After the fifteenth century discovery (easy for Americans to remember because of the famous year of discovery, 1492), trade, colonization, and conquest led to a virtual European takeover of the rest of the world. Now centuries later, students from widely dispersed national and ethnic points of origin sit together in the same college classroom. Do they share that space in peace and progress? Do they grow in knowledge of the roots of others and in an appreciation of their own roots? Can they pursue these inquiries through the curriculum? All should, of course, have some exposure to intercultural enrichment outside of class, through campus celebrations of ethnicity in food, art, and festival. But if nothing along these lines happens in class, so much the loss for them, so much the continuing leadership challenge for academic administrators.

RELEASING NATURE'S ENERGIES

All faculty have opportunities to enlist student participation in conversations about the impact of the various industrial, scientific, and technological revolutions that produced both the advancement and affluence that today's college students tend to take for granted. No discipline or course of studies should be excluded from these conversations; creative interdisciplinary cooperation can help make this kind of dialogue happen.

Philosophy and religious studies can raise the ethical and moral questions that have to be part of this humanizing conversation. Without the conversation, this generation of students will go sleepwalking into an unknown future. As a molecular biologist from the National Institutes of Health remarked not long ago, we are today, relative to the future of medicine, where Wilbur and Orville Wright were in 1903 relative to the future of air and space travel.

Nature's energies have indeed been released. We need to be talking more about the potential for good and ill that this release implies. Who calls the meeting, so to speak; who sets up the conversation, if not deans and the faculties they lead?

RULING OURSELVES

In the nineteenth century, the movement toward democratic government gained momentum. Gone were the earlier days of rule by kings and priests; broken was the link between inheritance and political power. No longer tenable was the premise that individuals existed for the state. Americans came to recognize in principle and in law universal rights for the individual.

American higher education well may be the best hope we have for success in using our freedoms well, exercising our rights responsibly, and ruling ourselves intelligently. But, again, it does not all happen in the classroom. Many students get their first real taste of the political process in those campus campaigns for election to positions in student government. These are wonderful laboratories for the examination and development of all the ingredients needed in a good campaign. Political rhetoric, polling, advertising, issue selection and analysis, campaign finance, getting out the vote—all this and more happens on virtually every college campus in America ever year. Chances are, it will be done well and responsibly if academic leaders work closely with the student-life professionals who manage the process.

Although it is pretty much out of fashion now, intramural and intercollegiate debating may stand a good chance of a comeback in the new tamer, and more compliant climate some observers see emerging on our campuses. A famous Washington lawyer once remarked to me that he had "cross-examined one thousand witnesses before ever going to law school; they called it high school and college debating!" And he went on to recall, at age fifty-nine, the lasting impact debating—and those who coached him in it—had on his life.

This essay has traversed an eight-stage development path from becoming human to ruling ourselves. At each stage, I've noted an opportunity and unique responsibility for academics to foster the growth of the human potential. This is essentially a question of how to become more fully human through the undergraduate experience.

THE UNCERTAIN FUTURE

In the third part of his book, David Fromkin offers four additional windows through which one can look out over the heads of currently enrolled students to the uncertain future that awaits them: "Anticipating What Comes Next," "Holding People Together," "Taking Nature's Place," and "Entering Yet Another American Century." Any range-finder can be used to size up the future. I would simply like to say to academics as they struggle to prepare for what might be next, that in this new American Century, things are not and never will be as bad as some would have you believe. So I sign off with these words from another historian, Gertrude Himmelfarb, who wrote in the *Wall Street Journal* (February 4, 1999):

> For almost every favorable statistic, an ornery conservative can cite an unfavorable one. He can even go beyond the statistics to point to the sorry state of the culture: the loss of parental authority and of discipline in the schools, the violence and vulgarity of television, the obscenity and sadism of rap music, the exhibitionism and narcissism of talk shows, the pornography and sexual perversions on the Internet, the binge-drinking and "hooking up" on college campuses. Two memorable phrases capture the cultural mood: Daniel Patrick Moynihan's "defining deviancy down," which normalizes and legitimizes what was once abnormal and illegitimate; and Roger Shattuck's "morality of the cool," which makes sin and evil seem "cool" and thus acceptable.

All in higher education have the challenge of (and the professional responsibility for) setting academic standards. In the process they will find themselves defining integrity *up*. Working through faculties to help students discover a morality that may be, at times, *uncool* (but that will always be courageous), academic leaders can help students grow in the conviction that the easy life is not the happy life, and that the life that is lived well is the life lived generously in service to others. If there is no evidence of this now on the academic side of the campus street, it isn't going to be there on the streets of life where the developing human potential of today's students will eventually unfold.

19

■

Styles of Social Involvement

Over the years—many years, fifty at least—I've thought a lot about styles and strategies of social involvement inspired by religious conviction. There is substance, of course, in the body of doctrine known as Catholic social teaching; there is also style. Moved by the principles of Catholic social teaching, one can become engaged directly or indirectly with the challenges presented by the problems that burden society and retard or suppress the development of human potential. There are also different models of social change.

Let me begin then with some thoughts about direct social involvement and, in that context, I'll use the notion of social work as a starting point. Social work, as a profession and academic discipline, can be conveniently divided into case work, group work, and community organizing. When applied to the direct social involvement of men and women of religious conviction, these three divisions might appear as sequential stages through which religious commitment can pass. But without abandoning any one stage, religious energy can target one or another stage with differing intensity as needs and times change.

From time to time, work with *cases* and specified problem *groups* can yield center stage to *community organizing* as a technique (and *community organizer* as an occupational title). This shift often goes by the name of *relevance* and occasionally encourages dismissive comments about band-aid solutions. This was fairly evident in the Roman Catholic community during the sixties and seventies as some religious men and women looked for a non-educational tool to use in serving the powerless poor, and others engaged in social analysis aimed at getting at the root causes of poverty. It also reflected a renewed confidence in participatory democracy, an awakening recognition of the presence of injustice in our midst, and an acceptance of the wisdom of serving people best by helping them to help themselves.

COMMUNITY ORGANIZING

Community organizing almost always implies argument, conflict, and confrontation. As a technique, it involves gaining the confidence of the community to be served, and isolating one issue—from the complaints expressed by members of the community—around which the community will organize itself for remedial or preventive action. After the organizing comes the confronting. Exploitation of the poor or racial minorities by, say, real estate agencies in changing neighborhoods would be what organizers call a good issue. Neighborhood safety and security issues, inadequate public services, discriminatory employment practices, and retail price-gouging are others. Individual members of the community are powerless to correct the injustice; but once they are organized around an issue that bothers them all, they have power—people power, if not the power of wealth—and with their power they have the possibility of change. With this comes the all-important sense of controlling their own destiny. And as a powerful sense of control is consciously felt, the oldest and weakest model of social change—fatalism—is set aside.

This has been happening in America over the past half century. Think back to the Black Power movement of the late sixties (offspring of the Black Nationalism movement associated with the name of Malcolm X). Not all community organizing efforts involve militancy, of course, but most do involve confrontation. A decade or so later, Latin American liberation theology emerged in Catholic conversations and both critics and defenders had to wrestle with the question of the use of violence as an instrument of social change.

The role of Catholic priest, nun, or religious brother in confrontational organizing activity is sometimes viewed as inappropriate. Their role is to work for the unification of the community under the impact of love. I'm not concerned here with a predictable right-wing critique from within religious communities of some of the direct ministries engaged in by some of their members who try to come to grips with the problems of racism, poverty, and war. "Where is the Gospel being preached in all of this?" these critics ask; "Let's don't turn into a bunch of social workers." These are often the same persons who ran the teen dances, produced plays, and coached athletics under specifically Catholic auspices in an effort to safeguard the morals of the young or build Christian character in decades past. Some have been overtaken by a myopic moral perspective that renders them unable or unwilling to see the Gospel being preached in the example of those who organize disadvantaged groups to combat injustice.

More enlightened criticism does, however, raise the question of possible inconsistency between the reconciliatory role of priests and religious and the conflict orientation of the community organizer. This question requires reflection and an honest examination of both motivation and means on the part of the organizer, but it is, of itself, hardly a disqualifier from a theological standpoint.

Still another criticism, or at least a reservation, suggests that intellectual talents capable of contributing to solid planning and long-term solutions might be wasted if direct action is a substitute for research and writing. This is a real danger and one to be kept in mind as we move now into a discussion of indirect social action, where I would include scholarly research, writing, teaching, and planning.

ACTIVISM VERSUS REFLECTION

A dominant theme in the social involvement of committed Catholics for about a century now has been the reconstruction or reform of the social order. It is significant, I think, that an American Catholic journal bearing the title *Social Order* is now long defunct. In one sense this signals a danger—the danger that activism can displace careful thought and our traditional Catholic social principles will not be articulated and applied to the concrete problems of our social order. There is a danger that Professor R.H. Tawney's (1926, 185) comment about a fifteenth-century Catholic failure might prove applicable to the American Church in the early decades of the twenty-first century: "The social teaching of the Church has ceased to count because the Church itself has ceased to think."

On the other hand, our evolving situation might be a sign of progress. Some of the best Catholic social thinkers are men and women working in secular agencies and universities. On this point, Jesuit theologian Karl Rahner's (1963, 32–33) essay on "Christians in the Modern World" is persuasive.

> We have a duty to take account of the fact, without any sense of shock, that the form of the Church's existence in public life is changing. The fact that the Church is becoming a diaspora everywhere, that she is a Church surrounded by non-Christians, and hence living in a culture, in a state, amidst political movements, economic activity, science and art which are conducted not simply and solely by Christians—all this is a *must* in the history of salvation. From this *must* we are permitted and indeed enjoined to draw sane and sober conclusions... for the offensive and defensive activities of the Church and of Christians.

To our surprise, and perhaps shock, Fr. Rahner asserts, "It is useless to commend our Christian principles to the world as its salvation. What it wants is to hear concrete proposals. We have got to have the courage to act as human beings with a task in the world of history, and so to come forward with such proposals. But we cannot propagate them in the name of Christianity" (15).

Note that he is contrasting Christian principles with proposals offered by Christians. Concretized, as it must necessarily be, a proposal is grounded in either good or bad economics, politics, social psychology, or whatever. Therefore, only a competent economist, political scientist, social psychologist, or other specialist can design the proposal. If he or she is a Christian, we might hope that Christian principles inspired him or her to gain the competence to produce the proposal. But Christian principles, as such, contribute nothing to the quality of the proposal.

In a paper, "Social Action in the American Environment," Edward Duff, S.J. (1959), then editor of *Social Order*, reminded the National Catholic Social Acton Conference: "We are committed to the reform of institutions, to changing the patterns of behavior and the conditions of existence that lessen the full measure of justice available to our fellow men." This goal must be sought, he said, in collaboration with other groups for the simple reason that we are a minority. And yet, Fr. Duff noted, "Catholics in this country are only beginning to work routinely with other groups."

From this small beginning considerable progress has been made in the ensuing decades. We see the rise of experts, who happen to be Catholic, working by conscious choice in secular institutions. We also see the decline of clerics and religious who, because they are Catholic, chose to acquire expertise in secular social sciences in order to work, through Catholic institutions, at the task of reforming institutions and changing behavior patterns—the task, in other words, of Christianizing the social order. A continuation of these trends will, I think, characterize religious social involvement into the indefinite future.

If the goal of Christianizing the social order sounds a bit like religious imperialism, I can only comment that it has certainly been taken that way by some of the would-be reformers themselves. This is not at all to say that we should not try to internalize Beatitude principles and the Pauline criteria, mentioned in earlier chapters, and carry them into our workplaces and other corners of our world. They do indeed have transformative value that is fully human as well as Christian.

NEIGHBORHOODS ARE NOT TO BE OVERLOOKED

It is possible that our preoccupation in the forties and fifties with saving the nation has, in a curious way, permitted us to stand by and lose our neighborhoods to the destructive forces of individualism, racism, and poverty. We still don't fully understand these forces. And in those poverty or urban ghetto areas where we still maintain an institutional presence (think of the so-called inner-city parishes), we continue to miss opportunities to improve the quality of life for *all* the neighborhood residents. At the levels of direct and indirect social involvement, our efforts now might better be focused on saving the neighborhoods, not the nation.

THE REFORM MODEL

The notion of social reform has developed in the Catholic mind to something of a battleground for conservative and liberal (or progressive) Catholics. Between World War II and the Second Vatican Council, the typical Catholic social reformer accepted the established institution (parish, school, hospital) in principle, but not necessarily in practice. He or she wanted to modify the institution but was not out to destroy it. This represented an advance over the passive, fatalistic model of social change I referred to earlier in this chapter.

The reform model involves planned change—long-range planning. It is congenial to bureaucracy and begins with at least an acceptance of (and often a commitment to) present structures. The next stage would be a model of revolution or discontinuous change. Before discussing the applicability of that model to our present situation, I want to comment on the reform model, since that is where most of us in the Church, individually and collectively, happen to be. It is basically a conservative position. It views progress as a planned development growing out of a tradition. Most of those who have been involved in parish, diocesan, or provincial planning—in the re-evaluation of old and the choosing of new ministries—will find a congenial starting point for thought about new social and apostolic ventures in these words of Henry George (1879, book 8, ch. 2): "It is an axiom of statesmanship, which the successful founders of tyranny have understood and acted upon, that great changes can best be brought about under old forms. We, who would free men, should heed the same truth. It is the natural method. When nature would make a higher type, she takes a lower one and develops it. This, also, is the law of social growth. Let us work by it. With the current we may glide fast and far. Against it, it is hard pulling and slow progress."

So here we are with multiple institutions and a bundle of questions as to how we can turn those institutions around (allowing for the elimination of some and the creation of new ones) to meet today's social problems. Henry George had a lot to say about land as an instrument of social reform. He respected the institution of private property and let it stand; he advocated, however, confiscatory taxation of rents derived from privately owned land. Analogously, socially-minded Catholics might consider retaining regard for education as an instrument, but set aside the notion that education must take place in a school room. Or coming at the same point in another way, we might learn a lesson from the railroads. The railroads long ago made the mistake of failing to recognize that they were in the transportation business. They considered as theirs only the narrow portion of that business that is tied to rails. Trucks, buses, and airlines, of course, came along to pass the railroads by. Institutionalized social reform that looks to education as an apt instrument cannot afford to let the understanding of education be too tightly tied to traditional tracks—classroom-centered, semester-spaced, degree-granting, child- and youth-focused, and separated from work experience.

IS THERE ROOM FOR REVOLUTION?

We in Catholic religious communities talk about changing style, opening up, and gaining institutional flexibility so that we might more effectively address ourselves to the issues of race, poverty, ecumenism, and peace (the list could run on!). But, if our membership statistics are reliable indicators, we don't seem to be changing fast enough. Perhaps we have not freed ourselves sufficiently from ministries designed to meet yesterday's problems. Whatever the reason, we have lost many members and have not yet attracted large numbers of new recruits.

Does the third model of social change have any relevance to all this? You will recall that the first was fatalism, the second was reform, and the third, now to be discussed, revolution. From the sit-ins in 1960, to the free speech movement at Berkeley in 1964, to the Selma march and Vietnam teach-ins of 1965, on to the resistance movement, the Catonsville Nine, the urban riots, the Children's Crusade, the 1968 Democratic National Convention in Chicago, and subsequent protest demonstrations, we witnessed in the decade of the sixties a rise in the radical spirit almost as dramatic as the fall of John and Robert Kennedy and Martin Luther King. Note, however, that it was a rise in the radical, not revolutionary spirit, and it was present both within and outside circles of religious influence.

The report on the first consultation on the future of the campus ministry, "Campus Ministry Faithfulness" (1970, 25–26) stipulated: "Revolution demands three preconditions: first there must be a large, widely shared reservoir of frustration and discontent; second, there must be a myth capable of capturing the imagination and identifying the major source of frustration while promising relief; third, there must be charismatic leadership capable of articulating the myth and mobilizing the reservoir of discontent and alienation on behalf of change."

These conditions never ripened in the sixties and show no signs of ripening now in America. As bad as things may seem, the conditions for real social revolution are just not there. This is not to say that there are no real revolutionaries on the religious and social scenes. To the extent that they are present—few as they are—in church circles, their presence is a sign that we can choose the future we want, and thus they are a sign of hope. Although outnumbered in seminaries and church-related colleges and universities by conservatives, they are visible in various movements—peace, the environment, hunger, immigration rights, and other social justice causes. They are for the most part activists, not theoreticians. Their tactic is non-violent, occasional (i.e., seasonal and episodic) direct action. They critique and resist what they judge to be institutionalized injustice. Some few want new systems, not just remodeled and reformed old ones, but they are not personally invested in building them.

To the extent that young radicals (not necessarily revolutionaries), lay or religious, can be found anywhere in organized Catholic life today, they want the Church to be a liberating and motivating environment, a base from which the Gospel, as they understand it, can be proclaimed in word and action (including institutional action), and social concerns, as they feel them, can be pursued. Their sense of moral outrage holds an enormous constructive potential for all of us, if they and we can prevent that moral outrage from turning into moralistic, self-righteous, and ideological intolerance. One can only speculate as to where Jesus would line up if he were in our midst today.

Our problem, however, is that there are not enough of the young radicals in our faith community, and those we have may not possess the staying power necessary to turn us all around for a more effective engagement with the social problems of our day. Moreover, those we have seem insufficiently committed to searching for intellectual solutions to present problems. My hope would be that we will witness an emergence of young individuarians in our midst, and that they will lead us into full engagement with the social problems of our time.

I have to say, however, that without thought, there will be no influence. Without intellect, there will be no good proposals. As Karl Rahner said, there are no Christian proposals; there are just good and bad proposals. Ours had better be good. They will have to have substance. And we will have to find the right style of social involvement to put those proposals on the tracks.

20

An Agenda for a Just Society

Just before leaving my job as dean of arts and sciences at Loyola University in New Orleans to become president of the University of Scranton in 1975, I published an article in *America* under the title "Seeking a Just Society: An Agenda for Americans." The editors, lifting some thoughts from the body of the article, inserted under the title this introductory note: "If we want a new social policy, we have to change our values. Caring for genuine needs must replace satisfying artificial cravings, and our ruthlessly competitive economy has to be humanized."

Shortly after arriving in Scranton, I was invited to give the keynote address at an event marking the launch of that year's United Way campaign in Lackawanna County. It occurred to me that the points I made in the *America* article would be just right for this speech to community-minded listeners who were ready to contribute time, talent, and treasure to a campaign aimed at meeting social welfare needs in the community. So I converted the article into a text for my speech and delivered it to a very receptive audience.

Particularly receptive was a young lawyer who, more than a decade earlier had traveled from Scranton to the Deep South to represent (pro bono) freedom riders and civil rights activists who were protesting the denial of voting rights to blacks. When I met him for the first time a few months later, Morey Myers told me he was shocked and pleasantly surprised to hear me—an academic administrator and a Catholic priest—proclaiming such progressive, even liberal ideas.

Thirty years later, when we were on a conference call discussing the Scranton seminar described in the opening chapter of this book, the article, "Seeking a Just Society: An Agenda for Americans" came up. Morey had recently reread it. Why not make the article a discussion paper for one of my sessions in the seminar? It was surely congenial to an "Individual and Society" theme. So the article was read and discussed after I had prepared the way with presentations on "The Principle of Human Dignity" and "Solidarity and the Common Good." What struck us all was the relevance of this 1975 essay to American society today. I offer it here, in its original form.

....

Reference points are needed to measure the distance between American social policy today and any future position to which a new policy might lead us. This essay will attempt no predictions of what, in fact, will happen. But the new social policy I have in mind will rest directly on an ethical foundation, on a *need-care* ethic. If the American conscience perceives the need and provides the care, a new social policy may develop. But first, the reference points.

Quite recently, I learned two new words: *Africare* and *Educare*. The first is the name of a new organization founded by a former Peace Corps volunteer. He is now a physician working directly with famine-stricken Africans. His organization hopes to go beyond medical-assistance efforts to include works aimed at the general improvement of the quality of life on the African continent. The objective is *Africare*.

Educare is a term destined to become popular as a new legislative goal emerges (after national health insurance is on the books) to provide educational rights for everyone who is covered by the Social Security system. That objective is down the road but on the way.

But where are we; where are we coming *from*, as we look ahead to Africare and Educare and other social- and societal-care objectives? We are at a self-enclosed point of preoccupation with skin care, clothes care, lawn care, floor care, appliance care, car care, and pet care. We are weight watchers, clock watchers, and girl watchers. We neglect our old and spoil our young. We pollute our air, poison our wells, and devour our non-renewable natural resources.

If challenged on any of these points, we justify ourselves as taxpayers, property owners, and free citizens in the richest and most powerful nation on earth. To protect our awesome accumulation of wealth and power, we approve expenditures for space exploration and national defense. To prevent a redistribution of wealth and income, and to preclude any significant re-distribution of power, we postpone true racial equality and staunchly oppose increased taxes on income, inheritance, or property. We also oppose foreign economic aid and welfare subsidies for the poor. In the trade-off between inflation and unemployment, we prefer higher joblessness to higher prices.

Subsidies and/or tax breaks for farmers, ship builders, oil producers, and countless other corporate enterprises enjoy our support as part of our continuing commitment to The System. Meanwhile, Educare and Africare and similar care-responses to social needs remain underfunded, or under wraps, or not even under consideration.

Paralleling our economic growth of the past thirty years has been a social process called *privatization*. With the rise of privatization, we have witnessed the weakening of community ties spinning off a new generation of isolated individuals, lonely and alienated, who turn to fantasy and sensate distractions as substitutes for social concerns and social action. This evident cultural tendency to withdraw from public action into a cocoon of privacy poses a danger to the social order and a challenge to social policy.

In *The Private Future*, Martin Pawley (1974, 8) writes:

> Western society is on the brink of collapse—not into crime, violence, or madness or redeeming revolution, as many would believe—but into withdrawal. Withdrawal from the whole system of values and obligations that has historically been the basis of public, community, and family life. Western societies are collapsing not from an assault on their most cherished values, but from a voluntary, almost enthusiastic

abandonment of them by people who are learning to live private lives of an unprecedented completeness with the aid of the momentum of a technology which is evolving more and more into a pattern of socially atomizing appliances.

I do not think Pawley's entire book is of any great value, but his early treatment of the privatization phenomenon is good. Withdrawal *is* the problem.

But why withdrawal? Is affluence the reason? Or is there something deeper, something beneath our beautiful skin that can explain our anxiety and restlessness, our cruelty and callousness, our lack of concern for the powerless, our unconscious complicity in evil? Why are we afraid? Why do we lack the creativity and commitment necessary to connect ourselves into a fulfilling human community? Apparently, we do not recognize what William Lynch has perceived, namely, that "the purely private is always ugly."

Pawley notes a "withdrawal from the whole system of values and obligations that has historically been the basis of public, community, and family life." He does not specify what that system is. One might assume that it is the Judaeo-Christian ethical tradition, even the Natural Law.

Anyone familiar with Natural Law ethics will recognize a relationship between right and obligation. If I possess a right, there is a corresponding obligation to exercise it properly. But there is also a relational obligation resident in you to respect my right. Similarly, I have a duty to recognize and respect your rights. Rights, in this vocabulary, are associated with personhood.

In the interest of establishing an ethical base for a new social policy, I insert into this vocabulary the notions of need and care. I would argue that a genuine human need constitutes a genuine human right. The human right derives from the human need. I would argue further that the capacity to care for a genuine human need constitutes a genuine human obligation. This is not to say that what you can do, you must do—thus opening the door to those moral imperative arguments that justify weapons development, genetic engineering, and other forms of exploration on the grounds that possession of the power implies the right to exercise it.

I am saying, however, that possession of the power to meet a genuine human need constitutes, in the face of that need, a moral obligation on the part of the possessor. The seriousness of the obligation depends on the seriousness of the need and on the proximity and capability of the person or group who can meet that need. Moreover, I would ground this need-care ethic in the Christian Gospel, not thereby to make it politically irrelevant, as has happened in the past, but to affirm the relevance of Gospel values for a new social policy. No new social policy will succeed without them. As a friend reminded me recently: Socrates said, "Know thyself." Freud said, "Be thyself." And Jesus said, "Give thyself." Social needs in America call for a mass migration of our people into that third stage.

There is a tendency among citizens in privatized America to prefer to live, not by principle, but by desire. When needs (not mere wants) are recognized as ethically significant and as the ground of principled choice, the cocoon of privatized, personal desire will open out toward social concerns. A new social obligation will be felt; new social action will follow. Recognition of the principles is clearly antecedent to the action. And detachment from privatized, self-enclosed desires is prerequisite to recognition of the human needs upon which the social-moral principles rest.

In order to recapture a sense of social-moral obligation, America may have to return to Plymouth Rock. We will have to recapture a sense of thanksgiving. James Gustafson sees a relationship between prayer and moral obligation, for prayer fosters a sense of gratitude. And without gratitude, obligation is impossible. *Much obliged* is not so vacant a phrase as its mindless repetition would suggest.

What are the needs to which our new social policy must address itself? There is the general need for personal, family, and community security, dignity, and peace. Particular needs relate to nutrition, shelter, health, education, employment, and cultural development.

Global needs relate to issues of population (both numbers and density), famine, war, and socio-economic development.

There is nothing new in the assertions that every person has a need (right) to live and eventually to die with dignity, a need (right) to eat, a need (right) to know, a need (right) to be clothed and housed, a need (right) to have health care, a need (right) to have productive employment, a need (right) to be free and seek self-fulfillment, a need (right) to love and be loved. But none of these rights is absolute, not even the right to life. Moreover, there are moral limits on the exercise of these rights, particularly the right to personal fulfillment.

Corresponding to these needs and rights are obligations elsewhere. Curiously, in the case of affluent America, these obligations are both resident in and largely unattended by those whose needs are adequately met.

To the extent that we acknowledge these obligations, our tendency in America has been to discharge them indirectly, through public or private agencies. Private contributions or public taxes (the former often deductible from the latter) finance the delivery of care to need. But this delivery system often disregards the personal dignity of the recipient and the personal identity of the donor, thus all but destroying any semblance of principled activity evoked by human need and grounded in a sense of moral obligation. With the awareness of these human relationships all but vanished from America, it is not surprising that a sense of family, neighborhood, and national community has gone too.

Agencies are necessary. Indirect payments are more often than not the only way one person can touch the most urgent needs of others. But whether managed the "United" way or by the various governmental tax-and-transfer mechanisms, our care-to-need delivery arrangements are simply inadequate. They require qualitative improvement by means of a heightened citizen awareness of the need-care ethic. They demand quantitative improvement made possible only by larger contributions from those who have more, to those who have less. The necessary contributions are not solely financial; they also involve educational and economic opportunity.

I happen to believe that a humanistic capitalism is still possible. Hence a considerably improved social policy can emerge from modifications of the present system. Not all agree with this. A radical critique would urge the destruction or dismantling of the system since the capitalist system, based as it is on competition (not cooperation) and personal greed (not generosity), *produces* the problems our new social policy would attempt to solve.

From another direction, the conservative critique would see government as the villain and deplore any more involvement by government in social policy. Unfettered private enterprise will generate social welfare, the argument goes; it has not yet worked because it has not yet really been tried.

It is always a mistake to substitute blame for analysis. The danger at the extreme left, as I see it, is the possibility that the human person will be ground under by the wheels of collectivism (once described in the London *Economist* as "the bureaucratic miscarriage of socialism"). On the right, the human person is likely to be the victim of a rugged individualism. Seeing ourselves in a Christian perspective as *loved sinners* (a phrase borrowed from the Jesuit psychologist William Barry), and retaining an awareness, in faith, that we are at once forgiven and yet in need of forgiveness, we can come upon the neither arrogant nor utopian middle ground of Christian humanism. This is personalist territory; it is also social. The Christian is reconciled to God in Christ, as we know. But the Christian is not reconciled as an isolated individual, nor as an unknown quantity in a faceless collectivity. God's new covenant with us is interpersonal, but with us only as persons-in-community. Thomas Clarke, S.J., the Woodstock theologian, came up with this idea a few years ago and applied it to the horizontal dimension of religious vows—a formal commitment to the religious community that "I'll be around." This insight has implications for the socio-political order, once we agree that moral obligation rests on those with the capacity to care. With the capacity, there ought to be a commitment to others who become identifiable by virtue of their need.

A humanistic capitalism or a personalistic socialism—either, I contend, is consistent with Christian principles, compatible with a need-care ethic, and workable in a human community weakened by original sin yet strengthened by the grace of Christ.

If you have it, you *have* to share. If you have *made it*, you have also picked up a new responsibility along with that quantifiable and presumably valuable *it*. I am not speaking of a legal responsibility because often there is none. I have in mind a moral responsibility. The two are not always the same. Let me offer an anecdote to demonstrate that the popular mind is often confused with regard to the importance of the two.

When the City of New Orleans was girding itself against the arrival of Hurricane Carmen on September 7, 1974 (the center of the storm eventually missed the city by a hundred miles), Mayor Moon Landrieu monitored preparation activities from his City Hall desk and the local television stations gave uninterrupted, round-the-clock, crisis coverage. Complaints of price gouging came to the Mayor as Carmen neared the Louisiana coast and prudent citizens sought supplies of batteries, transistor radios, candles, and canned goods. "Overcharging is not illegal, but it is unconscionable, particularly in a time of emergency," Landrieu declared to reporters as he urged people to report overcharging to his Office of Consumer Affairs. One of the television stations reported this particular news item in these words: "The Mayor has said these acts are not per se illegal, only immoral."

No suitable new social policy will gain acceptance in America until that priority is reversed, until the moral enjoys precedence over the legal in fact and in popular perception. Not everything that is moral is a matter of law, although law must in all cases be moral. Legal links will not hold a society together, even though a society without laws is not possible. Laws of themselves are insufficient to guarantee societal life. Better laws will contribute to a better society. Ideas for a new social policy will eventually have to find expression in law.

What are some of these ideas? I have already mentioned Educare and Africare. Those labels cover ideas that admit of legislative enlargement into programs of widespread continuing education at home and socio-economic aid abroad. Other areas to be touched by a new social policy are infant and child nutrition, population density, the integrity of the family unit, wage structures and income supplements, tax reform, racial discrimination, the criminal justice system, dependence and alienation, unemployment, the automobile, uses of mass communications, uses of technology; a new social policy should reward cooperation and foster international-mindedness.

I suspect that we have in America only the beginnings of the application of the insurance principle to social needs. Insurance against death, illness, unemployment, disability, fire, theft, and numerous other events or conditions that threaten human security is commonplace. The wealthy are well insured. Many of them become wealthy by insuring others. Through some creative applications of the insurance principle, inequality would be reduced and security would be enhanced. It amazes me to ponder the amount of human trust that makes our extensive banking system possible. I wonder if we have an adequate supply of human care to work out insurance systems against the emergence of many of the needs I have already mentioned. At the moment, we have not. We have instead the enormous task of working for radical change in our dominant values, thus releasing our great potential for care.

It is possible that such attitudinal change and value substitution may have already begun. Surely, something is happening in the American mind; it could be the beginning of a new capacity to care.

There was another time of value change, perhaps before the founding of our nation (I shall leave it to the historians of ideas to locate the era), when we began moving toward our present cultural dilemma. The present problem was identified by Willis W. Harman of the Stanford Research Institute in these words at a 1972 White House "Conference on the World Ahead":

> Contemporary political, military, economic, ecological, and social crises are reflections of an underlying moral and spiritual crisis of civilization, and their resolution depends upon the resolution of that deeper crisis. The underlying dilemma is that somehow humanistic and transcendental values have come to be a luxury superimposed on economic values, rather than being the measure of the appropriateness of economic values. The result is that, rather than reinforcing the best we know, the economic institutions of the society seem to be at odds with the society's highest values.

The possibility to be noted is that there is a new awareness in America that could lead us toward a new assimilation of old values—like justice and truth—thus opening the door to a new era where the deeper crisis may be resolved. Without value change, no new social policy will work. I do not agree with Garrett Hardin's (1968) position that appeals to conscience will be ineffective and that the only way to establish a better social policy is by "mutual coercion, mutually agreed upon." His phrase has undeniable appeal, however, because of its realism. But once you have mutual coercion, mutually agreed upon, you really have cooperation based on mutual and enlightened self-interest; the coercion stems not from the force of another will, but from the urgency of an outside problem. This reflects real progress in moral sensitivity and social concern.

Let me now list some points on an agenda toward a new social policy.

Nutrition. Guarantee proper nutrition to every child from conception until six years of age, and you will witness an extraordinary rise in academic achievement and a decline in criminal behavior.

Hunger. Organize the American conscience around the issue of world hunger, and you will see a rapid rise in moral sensitivity and an improved delivery system for food to the needy at home and overseas. Out of this will develop a sensible and human agricultural policy in the United States. In his keynote address to the UN conference on the world food crisis, held in Rome in November, 1974, Henry Kissinger, the U.S. Secretary of State, declared his nation's commitment to a decade of collaborative effort with other nations toward the goal of building a world where no child anywhere will go to bed at night hungry. Although he gave no particulars, this very announcement may prove to be a landmark in U.S. social policy. Or it could become another example of "Let them eat promises"—a phrase Nick Kotz (1969) chose as the title of his book about domestic hunger. For the record, in any case, here are Dr. Kissinger's words: "The profound promise of our era is that for the first time we may have the technical capacity to free mankind from the scourge of hunger. Therefore, today we must proclaim a bold objective—that, within a decade, no child will go to bed hungry, that no family will fear for its next day's bread and that no human being's future and capacities will be stunted by malnutrition." Global cooperation in food, the Secretary said, could be a model for cooperation in other areas, among them energy and protection of the environment.

Education. Improve the quality of schools; break the popular misconception that education happens only in school; diversify the learning communities, particularly with respect to age; guarantee equality of educational opportunity and pluralism of ideas; and you will witness the demise of prejudice and the reduction of poverty.

Population. Improve the economic status of the poor (at home and abroad) and the rate of population increase will decline. Reduce the density of population centers and you will measure the improved quality of life in terms of reduced crime and lower anxiety levels. Listen to the warnings of the demographers and take all necessary steps, moral and technological, to keep a balance between population growth and our physical life support systems.

Family. Strengthen the marriage bond and you will strengthen society. Guarantee women's rights but make it possible for mothers of children under eighteen years of age to exercise those rights by opting out of the labor market, if they want to, without doing economic damage to the family. We need a better system of family allowance than tax deduction for dependents now provides.

Housing. Recognize that housing, not busing, holds the key to the school integration issue and that housing follows economic opportunity. Like our cities, our housing must be designed to embody beauty and encourage the growth of human community.

Incomes. Whether guaranteed, subsidized, or controlled, all forms of income should be subject to the same treatment from the central government; this means wages, salaries, profits, interest, rents, and dividends. Income redistribution is at or near the top of the agenda for a new social policy. The job market is a totally inadequate device for income redistribution.

Taxes. To finance needed social and public services, taxes will have to go up.

Inflation. Productivity gains will have to be fostered by a new social policy but they should be shared with the consumer in the form of lower prices rather than translated directly into higher wages or higher profits. Non-polluting growth will ease inflationary pressures; so will simplified lifestyles. What Senator Mark Hatfield has called our "throw-away ethic" which praises convenience and disposability is, in fact, one of the present great threats to our future economic well-being.

Race. The sooner we admit that the decay of our cities, the decline of public services, and the rise of crime and various forms of addiction are not unrelated to our denial of rights and dignity to blacks, the sooner we will understand the roots of our so-called urban crisis.

Justice. Within the criminal justice system (police, courts, prisons) the corrections system represents the social institution that is closest to revolution in America today. No new social policy can afford to ignore this possibility. Prison reform will involve human understanding between those who live in prison and those who work there, humane containment for dangerous, potentially violent convicts, and new out-of-prison rehabilitation programs for property offenders. Society would be better off if approximately 70 per cent of its present prison population were released to non-punitive community rehabilitation centers.

Alienation. This unconnected and unhappy state is rooted in materialism. It can only get worse if our values do not change.

Automobiles. Their appetites for concrete, asphalt, petroleum, and other natural resources will have to be curbed. Social controls on their size and use will have to be accompanied by creative alternatives to private and privatizing means of transportation. To the extent that the automobile tends to be used to compensate for psychological deficits in the American character, we might learn a lot about ourselves by observing how and why, and when and where we drive our cars.

Communications. The Cary Grants and Jimmy Stewarts of the seventies are Roger Mudd and John Chancellor. The closest thing we have now to the reassuring tones of FDR is the voice of Walter Cronkite. Eric Sevareid is the two-minute, thrice-a-week, secular substitute for the thirty-minute Sunday sermon. We live now in an electronic community, in touch, literally, with fewer people, but in contact with the world. Television has changed our politics, our entertainment and reading habits, and countless other aspects of our lives. After study of what has happened to us through our televiewing, our new social policy will have to deal with television as a tool, not a toy, capable of communicating to the public information about many of the elements of our need-care ethic, particularly the extent and urgency of our societal needs.

Technology. Our new social policy will have to control the uses of technology. Non-polluting growth will be a challenge to our brainpower as well as to our value system. The conversion of solar energy into economically feasible use for rich and poor should be high on our social agenda. Our successful national effort to put a man on the moon by 1970 should be matched by another decade of national commitment to develop solar energy systems. The poor nations do not have great underground energy sources, but they all do get their share of the sun. Healthcare—made possible, to an extent heretofore undreamed of, by our new technology—must be made available, to those who need it, by our new social policy.

International-mindedness. The only two-word term in this sixteen-point agenda for the new social policy is one that must dominate our need-care outlook. Africare is a step in that direction. Cooperation must be international in scope. Trade must respect comparative advantage and resist imperialistic and exploitive tendencies. Aid will have to increase, but trade is more important. If all our points are attended to in a context of international-mindedness, peace—the greatest human need—will be a possibility.

The outcome of the social policy outlined here will be the socialization of learning, of property, of opportunity, and of power. It is all a matter of degree. I repeat what I mentioned earlier, namely, that I think a humanistic capitalism is still possible. I'm not sure, however, how long it will remain a true possibility. And another footnote that should be appended to this or any other social agenda is the reminder that not every public responsibility has to be governmentally implemented.

Our last best hope for a new social policy may lie in Educare, a commitment to build a *learning* society. The educated society stands a good chance of becoming, in fact, a just society. Mark Twain used to complain that youth was such a wonderful thing it is regrettable that we waste it on young people. Similar observations could be made about education. It might provide mature America with the best route toward a new social policy.

There is a Chinese saying to the effect that if you are planning for a year, plant rice; if you are planning for a decade, plant trees; but if you are planning for a century, educate your people.

. . . .

As I mentioned, the seminar participants were struck by the relevance of this agenda for the present day. The paper provoked excellent discussion. With the paper as a benchmark, I asked the participants to respond to the following question. *What do you see as the most significant issue today's collegiate generation is going to have to deal with over the course of its collective lifetime?* I asked them to understand *significant* to mean not necessarily *most urgent* or *immediately pressing*, but instead to think of it as referring to the issue that, if attended to, has the best chance of assuring that there will be a just society in America fifty or sixty years from now—the estimate of the years remaining—the collective lifetime—for today's collegians. Conversely, if unattended, the issue might point to the dissolution or death of our society, if not our world.

Understandably, a long and fairly predictable list of candidates for *most significant issue* was generated by this thoughtful group. I'll close by mentioning only one—materialism—which, if left unattended, is certain to stifle our spirit, erode our values, and destroy our intellectual capacity to come up with solutions to the problems we will surely face. Those problems await us on the technological, political (and geo-political), diplomatic, medical, economic, psychological, scientific, and spiritual fronts. For it is in the arena of immateriality—spirit, thought, imagination, creativity, and love—that we will find the tools to preserve our dignity and forge our future.

Origins and Acknowledgments

Chapter One, "An Individuarian Outlook," grew out of discussions in an adult education seminar at the University of Scranton in February and March, 2006. The individuarian theme was originally developed in chapter eight of my book *Jesuit Saturdays: Sharing the Ignatian Spirit with Lay Colleagues and Friends* (Chicago: Loyola Press, 2000).

Chapter Two, "The Beatitudes and Catholic Social Thought," draws on lectures I've given to various audiences; the ten principles of Catholic Social Teaching that constitute the core of this chapter originally appeared as "Ten Building Blocks of Catholic Social Teaching," *America* 179, no. 13 (October 31, 1998), 9–12.

Chapter Three, "An Attitude of Gratitude," appears in a shorter and revised version in *St. Anthony Messenger* Vol. 114, no. 12 (May 2007).

Chapter Four, "Looking to the Year 2050," is a response to an invitation I received to assist the British Jesuits in planning for their future. Parts of this chapter were given at St. Edward's University in Austin, Texas on November 16, 2004 in the Bishop John E. McCarthy Forum on the Catholic Church in the Third Millennium.

Chapter Five, "A Church in Crisis," is an expansion of several lectures and an article first published in *Church* Magazine under the title, "Structural Adjustments for a Church Working Its Way through Crisis" (Winter 2004). This article won a first place Best Essay award from the Catholic Press Association.

Chapter Six, "Protecting Children from Pornography on the Internet," is an outgrowth of work done, 2000–02, on a Federal Commission charged with producing a report under the title of "Tools and Strategies to Protect Kids from Pornography on the Internet" (National Academy of Sciences). A summary article appeared in *St. Anthony Messenger* 110, no. 12 (May 2003), 28–33.

Chapter Seven, "Organizational Ethics," is based on a presentation to the Catholic Health Association meeting in Chicago, June 7, 2004, and later incorporated into my book *The Power of Principles: Ethics in the New Corporate Culture* (Maryknoll, NY: Orbis Books, 2006).

Chapter Eight, "Courage and Competence," is derived from conversations in several Woodstock Business Conference meetings and from a lecture sponsored by the Garaventa Center at the University of Portland on June 4, 2005.

Chapter Nine, "Reasoned Argument about Abortion," has origins in many conversations with scholars and politicians. A shorter version appeared as "Prolife & Prochoice: Can the Democrats Enlarge Their Tent?" *Commonweal* 132, no.3 (February 11, 2005), 9–10.

Chapter Ten, "Seeking Justice, Ending Hunger," draws on many talks in many places about the Christian citizens' lobby, Bread for the World, but in this case it was an address to the New Mexico chapters of Bread for the World, assembled in Albuquerque on September 18, 2004.

Chapter Eleven, "Geno Baroni," is a tribute to a great social-action priest who died all too young. Friends and colleagues gathered in Washington on October 24–25, 2005 to mark what would have been his seventy-fifth birthday and to celebrate his life while recalling the principles by which he lived it.

Chapter Twelve, "Social Justice Education," originated in lectures at Boston College and Marywood University. An alternate version appeared in *Integrating the Social Teaching of the Church into Catholic Schools: Conversations in Excellence 2000*, proceedings of a July 8, 2000 seminar at Boston College sponsored by the National Catholic Educational Association.

Chapter Thirteen, "Wealth and Responsibility," originated as a response to the editors of the *National Catholic Reporter* to contribute to a special supplement (March 11, 2005) on the theme: "Putting Your Money Where Your Faith Is."

Chapter Fourteen, "The Good Life," originated in drafts of a strategic plan for Georgetown University and eventuated in the form of an address to the graduates of the University of Portland, May 2, 2004.

Chapter Fifteen, "Workplace Spirituality," had its origins in articles and talks that I've delivered on this theme over the years, beginning with "Spirituality for the Workplace," *Spiritual Life* 44, no. 2 (Summer 1998), 67–75. For more than a decade, I've facilitated chapter meetings of the Woodstock Business Conference, a network of prayer-and-discussion groups in about a dozen cities, all with the single purpose of affirming the relevance of religious faith to business practice.

Chapter Sixteen, "Spirituality and the Social Question," is a revised version of an article by the same title that I wrote for *Chicago Studies* 38, no.3 (Fall/Winter 1999), 329–38.

Chapter Seventeen, "Religion and Politics," reflects countless conversations as well as lectures and articles on this topic which has been a long-standing interest of mine.

Chapter Eighteen, "Becoming Ever More Human," was first developed as a lecture for a convention of academic administrators. This present form reflects discussion and debate on the points covered in this chapter with faculty friends at Georgetown and at Loyola University of New Orleans.

Chapter Nineteen, "Styles of Social Involvement," is rooted in the social turmoil of the sixties. It first took shape as a presentation made at the University of Dayton on June 24, 1970 to the thirteenth annual assembly of the Conference of Major Superiors of Religious Men. That text appeared under the title, "Social Involvement and American Religious Life," in *Catholic Mind (The Monthly Review of Christian Thought)* 68, no.1157 (November 1970) 14–23. I saw that period as "turnaround time" in American religious life and noticed that the social forces then at work, which I've followed in subsequent lectures and writing, had relevance in secular institutional settings as well.

Chapter Twenty, "An Agenda for a Just Society," originated, as I acknowledge in the text, in my 1975 *America* article, " 'Seeking a Just Society': An Agenda for Americans." Its continuing relevance explains my participation in the 2006 seminar described in the introduction to this book. In one sense this is discouraging, since it points to so much that has not yet been done. On the other hand, it is encouraging to note that there is still a good deal of interest in a new, but not altogether different society, in activating a need-care ethic on the way to a more just society.

References

Arrupe, Pedro, S.J. 1986. *One Jesuit's spiritual journey: Autobiographical conversations with Jean-Claude Dietsch, S.J.* St. Louis: Institute of Jesuit Sources.

Branch, Taylor. 2006. *At Canaan's edge: America and the King years, 1965–68.* New York: Simon & Schuster.

Byron, William J., S.J. 1998. "Ten building blocks of Catholic social teaching." *America* (October 31).

———. 2000. *Jesuit Saturdays.* Chicago: Loyola Press.

———. 2006. *The power of principles: Ethics in the new corporate culture.* Maryknoll, NY: Orbis Books.

"Campus ministry faithfulness." 1970. *The Professional Identity of the Campus Minister.* Cambridge, MA: The Church Society for College Work.

Catechism of the Catholic Church. 1992. Washington: USCC Publishing Services.

Covey, Steven R. 1989. *Seven habits of highly effective people.* New York: Simon & Schuster.

D'Antonio, Michael. 2006. *Hershey: Milton S. Hershey's extraordinary life of wealth, empire and utopian dreams.* New York: Simon & Schuster.

Davis, Paul. 2005. "Outsourcing can make sense but proceed with caution." *Chronicle of Higher Education* (January 28).

Diamond, Jared. 2005. *Collapse: How societies choose to fail or succeed.* New York: Viking.

Douglas, Mary, and Steven Ney. 1998. *Missing persons: A critique of personhood in the school sciences.* Berkeley and Los Angeles: Univ. of California Press.

Duff, Edward, S.J. 1959. "Social action in the American environment." *Social Order* 9:7 (September).

Dunn, Kenneth. 2004. (In an interview with Mica Schneider). *Business Week* (March 29).

Friedman, Thomas L. 2005. *The World is Flat.* New York: Farrar, Straus and Giroux.

Fromkin, David. 1999. *The way of the world: From the dawn of civilizations to the eve of the twenty-first century.* New York: Alfred A. Knopf.

Fukuyama, Francis. 1995. *Trust: The Social Virtues and the Creation of Prosperity.* New York: Free Press.

George, Bill. 2003. *Authentic Leadership: Rediscovering the Secrets to Creating Lasting Value.* San Francisco: Jossey-Bass.

George, Henry. 1912. *Progress and Poverty.* Garden City, NY: Doubleday, Page & Co. (Orig. pub. 1879.)

Goffee, Robert, and Gareth Jones. 2000. "Why should anyone be led by you?" *Harvard Business Review* (September–October).

Golin, Al. 2003. *Trust or Consequences: Build Trust Today or Lose Your Market Tomorrow.* New York: American Management Association.

Goodwin, Doris Kearns. 2005. *Team of Rivals: The Political Genius of Abraham Lincoln.* New York: Simon & Schuster.

Greenleaf, Robert K. 1983. *Servant Leadership: A Journey into the Nature of Legitimate Power and Greatness.* New York: Paulist Press

Hardin, Garrett. 1968. "Tragedy of the Commons." *Science* (December 13).

Hooper, Leon, S.J. 1995. "Citizen Murray." *Boston College Magazine* (Winter).

John Paul II. 1981. *Laborem exercens.*

Lowenstein, Roger. 2004. *Origins of the Crash.* New York: Penguin Press.

Mahar, Maggie. 2004. *Bull!: A History of the Boom and Bust, 1982–1999.* New York: Harper Business.

McDermott, Alice. 1998. *Charming Billy.* New York: Farrar, Straus & Giroux.

Murphy-O'Connor, Jerome, O.P., contrib. 1990. *The New Jerome Biblical Commentary.* Upper Saddle River, NJ: Prentice Hall.

O'Malley, John W., S.J. 1993. *The First Jesuits.* Cambridge, MA: Harvard Univ. Press.

O'Rourke, Larry. 1991. *Geno.* New York: Paulist Press.

Pawley, Martin. 1974. *The Private Future.* New York: Random House.

Pontifical Council for Justice and Peace. 2004. *Compendium of the social doctrine of the Church.* Rome: Libreria Editrice Vaticana.

Rahner, Karl. 1963. "Christians in the modern world." *The Christian Commitment: Essays in Pastoral Theology.* New York: Sheed & Word.

Reflections. 1998. *Sharing Catholic Social Teaching: Challenges and Directions; Reflections of the U.S. Catholic Bishops.* (Also includes *The summary report of the task force on Catholic social teaching and Catholic education.*) http//www.usccb.org/sdwp/projects/socialteaching/ socialteaching.htm.

Reichardt, Joanne DeLavan. 2003. "Corporate America's new secret weapon: Trust." *The Public Relations Strategist* (Fall).

Riesman, David. 1954. Individualism reconsidered and other essays. Glencoe, IL: The Free Press.

Ryan, Desmond. 1986. *The Catholic Parish.* London: Sheed & Ward.

Summary. (See *Reflections*).

Tawney, R.H. 1926. *Religion and the Rise of Capitalism.* New York: Harcourt Brace.

Wuthnow, Robert. 1998. *After Heaven: Spirituality in America since the 1950s.* Berkeley: Univ. of California Press.

Youniss, James, and Miranda Yates. 1997. *Community Service and Social Responsibility in Youth.* Chicago: Univ. of Chicago Press.

Youth, Pornography, and the Internet. 2002. Washington: National Academy Press. www.nap.edu.

Index

A
abortion, 89–93, 111–112, 153–154
Abraham, 98
activism, 169–171
Africare, 178–179
After Heaven: Spirituality in America Since the 1950s, 142–143
agenda, 14–16, 147
Albuquerque, New Mexico, 95
alienation, 188
Ambrose, Saint, 15
America in the King Years, 4
America (magazine), 18, 28, 43, 114–115, 177
Amos, 115–116
Analects of Confucius, 134
Aquinas, Thomas, Saint, 15
Aristotle, 113
Arrupe, Pedro, 37
Arthur Andersen, 65
association, 11, 15
At Canaan's Edge, 4
attitude, 20–23
Auburn University, 71
Authentic Leadership, 81
authority, 39
automobiles, 189

B
Barker, David G., 38–41
Baroni, Geno, 103–112
Barry, William, 183
Basil the Great, 131
Beatitudes, 7–9, 22, 152–153
Beckmann, David, 100
becoming human, 155–165

Bernardin, Joseph, 15, 51, 122
BFW (Bread for the World), 95, 97–98, 100–102, 124
Black Nationalism, 168
Black Power movement, 168
Boston, Massachusetts, 46
Boston University, 71
Branch, Taylor, 4
Bread for the World (BFW), 95, 97–98, 100–102, 124
Britain, Church in, 38–44
Brown University, 125
Buffet, Warren, 83
Burghardt, Walter, 80–81
Burke, James E., 61–62, 66–67
Bush, George W., 107, 109
Business Week, 65, 109–110

C
Camp Dudley, 62–63
Campion College, 38
Carnegie Mellon, 73
Carter, Jimmy, 89, 103, 111
Carter, Rosalynn, 89
Casey, Robert P., 89–91, 93
Catechism of the Catholic Church, 10, 16
Catholic Church, future of, 29–44
Catholic education, 1, 6, 133–137
Catholic Health Association, 61–62
Catholic Parish, The, 39
Catholic University of America, The, 125
Catholic Worker Movement, 121
celibacy, 51–53
Chancellor, John, 189

character, personal, 56–58
Charming Billy, 140
Chavez, Cesar, 121
Cheek, Joey, 5
Chicago, Illinois, 61–62, 145–147
children, 55–60
Christ Jesus, 7–8, 10, 21–24, 52, 134, 136, 146, 151, 181, 183
Christians, Catholic, 7
Chronicle of Higher Education, The, 71
Chrysostom, John, 15, 131
Civic Responsibility and Higher Education, 127
civilization, 159–160
Clarke, Thomas, 183
Clement of Alexandria, 131
Clinton, Bill, 89, 109
Clinton, Hillary, 89
Collapse: How Societies Choose to Fail or Succeed, 6
commitment, 34–35, 67
Common Cause, 96
common good, 13–15, 68, 119–120
communications, 189
communism, 2
communitarianism, 2, 14, 125
community organizing, 168–169
community service, 2, 125–127
Community Service and Social Responsibility in Youth, 125
Compendium of the Social Doctrine of the Church, 131
competence, 33–34, 77–87
competition, 5–6
complacency, 39
Confucius, 134
Congregation of Holy Cross, 135
conscience, 160–161
cooperation, 5–6
corporate culture, 61–76
Corinthians I, Letter to the, 25–28
Coughlan, John, 82

Council of Independent Colleges, 155–165
Council of Trent, 40
courage, 77–87
Covey, Stephen R., 60
credenda, 14–16, 147
criminal penalties, 91–92
Cronkite, Walter, 189
Cross, the, 18

D
D-day, 74
D'Antonio, Michael, 4
Davis, Thurston, 43
Davis, Paul, 85–86
Day, Dorothy, 15, 121
Dead Man Walking, 122
dependence, 39
Deuteronomy, 30
Diamond, Jared, 6
dignity, 10–11, 15, 67
diversity, 152–153
divisions, 25–28
Douglas, Mary, 2
Drinan, Robert, 37–38
Droel, Bill, 145
Duff, Edward, 171
Duffy, Eammon, 40
Duke University, 85
Dunn, Kenneth, 73

E
Ebbers, Bernard, 77–80
Economist, 183
Educare, 178–179
education, college level, 155–165
education, moral, 155–165
education, social justice, 113–127, 187
Ehrlich, Thomas, 127
emptying, 22
England, Church in, 29–44
English Catholics, 38–44
Enron, 3, 65, 80–81

environmental concerns, 5–6, 12–13, 130
equality, 13, 15
Eucharist, 18–28, 120–121, 153
Everdell, William R., 157
Exodus, 24

F
fairness, 67
family, 187
Farm Street, 38
FEMA (Federal Emergency Management Administration), 110
First Amendment issues, 56–60, 107
First Jesuits, The, 29–30
freedom, 136–137, 163–164
Freud, Sigmund, 181
Friedman, Thomas, 5
Friendship 7, 21
Fromkin, David, 157–158, 164
Fukuyama, Francis, 73–74
future, choosing of, 29–44

G
Galatians, Letter to the, 127, 141–142
Gardner, John, 96, 155
Genesis, 98
Geno, 104
George, Bill, 81
George, Henry, 172–173
Georgetown University, 79
Gilby, Thomas, 93, 154
Glenn, John, 20–21
Global Positioning System, 146
Goffee, Robert, 49
Golin, Al, 73
Goodwin, Doris Kearns, 3
Gospel of Luke, 8
Gospel of Mark, 151
Gospel of Matthew, 7–8, 12, 152
Gospel of Work, 145–147
Goulet, Dennis, 48–49, 72
government policy, 41–42

governance, 81–83
Granger-Banyard, Peter, 135–136
gratitude, 17–28, 181
Greene, Graham, 37
Greenleaf, Robert, 80
Gregory the Great, 131
groupism, 2–3
"Guess Who's Coming to Dinner?", 20
Gustafson, James, 181

H
Hardin, Garrett, 186
Harman, Willis W., 185
Harvard Business Review, 49
Hatfield, Mark, 188
healthcare organizations, Catholic, 61–76
Hellwig, Monika, 111–112
Hershey, Milton S., 3–4
Hershey: Milton S. Hershey's Extraordinary Life of Wealth, Empire, and Utopian Dream, 4
Heschel, Abraham Joshua, 117
Heythrop, 38
Hillel, Rabbi, 134
Himmelfarb, Gertrude, 165
Holy Communion, 18–28, 120–121, 153
Holy Spirit, 127, 141–142
Holy Trinity, Washington, D.C., 23, 97–98
homosexuality, 52
Hooper, Leon, 106, 111
Hopkins, Gerard Manley, 37
housing, 187
Huckleberry Finn, 122–123
human dignity, 67
human life, 11, 15
human person, 10–11, 15
humanness, development of, 155–165
hunger, 95–102, 124, 186–187
Hurricane Carmen, 184
Hurricane Katrina, 110

I

Ignatius Loyola, Saint, 30, 36, 139, 143
incomes, 188
individualism, 1, 3, 11, 14
individuarian, 1–6, 124–125
inflation, 188
integrity, 67, 69
intelligence, 69
Inter-Religious Coalition of New York Clergy, 95–96
International Eucharistic Congress, 18, 20
international-mindedness, 189–190
Internet, 55–60
Iraq, 5

J

Jesuit ministries, 29–44
Jesuit Saturdays, 1
Jesuits, 1–2, 6
John Paul II, 52, 120, 122, 145
John XXIII, 106, 148
Johnson, Elmer W., 84–85
Johnson & Johnson, 61–62
Jones, Gareth, 49
Jordan, Vernon, 82
justice, 114–127, 177–191
Justice Sunday, 109–110

K

Keneally, Thomas, 66
Kennedy, John F., 174
Kennedy, Robert, 174
kenosis, 22
King, Martin Luther, Jr., 3–4, 122, 174
Kirkland & Ellis, 84–85
Kissinger, Henry, 186–187
Kotz, Nick, 186
Krugman, Paul, 70

L

Lackawanna County, 177
Landrieu, Moon, 184
Laodicea problem, 39
Lay, Ken, 80
leadership, 47–50, 68–70
Leo XIII, 147
life, respect for, 11, 15
Lincoln, Abraham, 3–4
Lippert, Peter, 30, 35
(London) Sunday Times Magazine, The, 43
Lonergan, Bernard, 62
loneliness, 43–44
love, 68, 134–136
Lowenstein, Roger, 70, 83
Loyola University, 177
Luke, 8

M

Mahar, Maggie, 70
Mahoney, Jack, 39
Malcolm X, 168
Marists, 38
Mary, mother of Jesus, 135–136
Matthew, 7, 12, 22, 52
McDermott, Alice, 140
meal, Eucharist as, 19–20, 23–28
Medtronic, 81
Mexico City, Mexico, 120
Millennium Challenge Account, 101
Milton S. Eisenhower Foundation, 103
money, 53–54
Montgomery bus boycott, 121–122
Month, The, 38
Moynihan, Daniel Patrick, 165
Mudd, Roger, 189
Mulchay, Anne, 5
Murphy-O'Connor, Jerome, 26
Murray, John Courtney, 30, 80–81, 93, 105–106, 110–111, 154
Murtha, Jack, 5
Myers, Morey, 177–178

N

Nadal, Jerome, 29–30, 34
NASA, 20–22

National Catholic Reporter, 37
National Center for the Laity, 145–147
National Conference of Catholic Bishops (NCCB), 9–16
National Institutes of Health, 153
National Press Club, Washington, DC, 100, 111
Navarro, Carlos, 95
NCCB (National Conference of Catholic Bishops), 9–16
neighborhoods, 171–172
New Jerome Biblical Commentary, The, 26
New Orleans, Louisiana, 184
New York, New York, 95–96
New York Times, The, 156–157
Newman, John Henry, 37–38
Ney, Steven, 2
nutrition, 186

O
O'Connor, Flannery, 124
O'Malley, John W., 29–30
O'Neill, Tip, 153–154
organizational ethics, 61–76
Origins of the Crash, 83
O'Rourke, Larry, 104, 106
"Our Town," 51
outsourcing, 85–86
Oxford, England, 29–44

P
Pacem in Terris, 148
parental involvement, 58–60
Parks, Rosa, 121–122
participation, 11–12, 15, 67, 82–87
Paschal Mystery, 74
Paul, Saint, 21–22, 25–28, 30, 34, 54, 127, 141–142
Paul VI, 123–124, 147
Pauline criteria, 141–142, 146–148
Pawley, Martin, 179–180
peace, 161

Peace Corps, 178
pedophilia, 45–54
Penn State University, 152
per capita human output, 6
Peter, Saint, 52
Philadelphia, Pennsylvania, 18
Philippians, Letter to the, 21–23
Plato, 113
Poitier, Sidney, 20
politics, 151–154
Pontifical Council for Justice and Peace, 131
poor, the, 12, 120–121
population, 187
Populorum Progressio, 147
pornography, 55–60
poverty, 96–99, 123–125
Power of Principles, The: Ethics in the New Corporate Culture, 68
practice-oriented spirituality, 142–143
preference for the poor, 15, 120–121
Prejean, Helen, 122
presidential elections, U.S. 2004, 8
PriceWaterhouseCoopers, 86
priesthood, 40
priests, quality of, 47–50
principles, Catholic social, 8–16
principles, ethical organizational, 67–68
principles, of Geno Baroni, 104–105
Private Future, The, 179–180
privatization, 179–180
protection, 12
Protestant Union Theological Seminary, New York, 95
Psalms, 130
Public Relations Strategist, The, 64

Q
Queen's College, 38
Queen's Foundation, 38

R
race, 188
Rahner, Karl, 81, 170, 175
Ranstad North America, 64
rationality, 161–162
reflection, 169–171
Reflections of the U.S. Catholic Bishops, 13–14
reform, 172–175
Regan, Ronald, 74
Reichardt, Joanne DeLavan, 64
"Religious-Based College and University Perspective, A," 127
respect for life, 11, 15
responsibility, 129–132
Riesman, David, 2–3
Roach, John R., 9
Romans, Letter to the, 97
Roosevelt, Franklin Delano, 118–119
Roosevelt, Theodore, 65
Ryan, D., 39

S
sacrifice, 18
same-sex marriage, 92
Saporito, Tom, 80
Sarah, 98
Sarbanes-Oxley, 79, 83
Second Vatican Council, 19, 105–106, 119, 172
Sermon on the Mount, 23
servant leadership, 50–54
Servant Leadership, 80
Seven Habits of Highly Effective People, The: Restoring the Character Ethic, 60
sex-abuse scandal, 45–54, 64–65
Seymour, Karen Patton, 70
Sharing Catholic Social Teaching: Challenges and Directions, 9–16
Shattuck, Roger, 165
Sheehan, Cindy, 5
Simon, Arthur, 95–96, 100

Simon, Paul, 96
Simon Peter, 145
Smiley, Jane, 139
social justice education, 113–127
Social Order, 169–171
social question, 145–149
social teaching, Catholic, 9–16, 132, 167–165
social values, 40, 68
social work, 167–175
society, seeking just, 177–191
Society of Jesus, 29–44
Socrates, 181
solidarity, 12, 15
Soviet Union, 20
spirituality and the social question, 145–149
St. John's Monastery, 51
stewardship, 12–13, 15, 130–132
Stewart, Martha, 70
Stimmen der Zeit, 30
subsidiarity, 13, 15, 68, 108–109, 118–119
Sullivan, Scott, 77–78

T
Tablet, The, 38
Tawney, R.H., 170
taxes, 188
Team of Rivals: The Political Genius of Abraham Lincoln, 3
technology, 189
Teresa, Mother, 15, 122
Thompson, Francis, 37
Thornburgh, Richard (Dick) L., 55–56, 77–80
Thousand Acres, A, 139–140
To Kill a Mockingbird, 134
Tolstoy, Leo, 3–4
Trinity Lutheran Church, New York, 95
trust, 61–76
Trust: The Social Virtues and the Creation of Prosperity, 73–74

trust bank, 73–75
Trust or Consequences: Build Trust Today or Lose Your Market Tomorrow, 73
Turin, Italy, 5
Twain, Mark, 122–123, 190
Tylenol, 61–62

U
union, 27–28
United States Conference of Catholic Bishops (USCCB), 9–16
United Way, 177
University of Georgia Foundation, 71
University of Idaho, 71
University of London, 38
University of Notre Dame, 84
University of Pennsylvania, 38
University of Portland, 77, 133–137
University of Scranton, 1, 177–178
USCCB (United States Conference of Catholic Bishops), 9–16

V
veracity, 67
virtues, Pauline, 127, 141–142
vocations, 31–44
vulnerable, the, 12

W
Walter Reed Hospital, 5
Washington, D.C., 5, 55–56, 100, 103, 111, 118–119
Way of the World, The: From the Dawn of Civilizations to the Eve of the Twenty-first Century, 157–158
wealth, 129–132
Welch, Jack, 69
Westport, NY, 62–63
Wharton School of Business, 38, 45
Whitehead, Alfred North, 37
Wilder, Thornton, 51
Williamsburg, Virginia, 155
Winter Olympics 2006, 5
withdrawal, 179–180
Wolfensohn, James, 100–101
women, 51–53, 74, 148, 187
Woodstock College, 30
Woodstock Theological Center, 79–81, 95
work, 12
workplace spirituality, 139–143, 145–149
World Bank, 100
World Is Flat, The, 5
WorldCom, 77–81
Wright, Orville, 153
Wright, Wilbur, 153
Wuthnow, Robert, 142–143

X
Xerox, 5

Y
Yates, Miranda, 125–127
Youniss, James, 125–127

About the Author

William J. Byron, S.J. is on leave from his position as research professor in the Sellinger School of Business at Loyola College in Maryland to serve as president of St. Joseph's Preparatory School in Philadelphia. He was president of the University of Scranton, 1975–1982, The Catholic University of America, 1982–1992, and was interim president of Loyola University in New Orleans, 2003–2004.